Strick-ly Socks

Wishing you a happy Strick-ly Socks

Candace Cisneros Smith

Strick-ly Socks

A Revolutionary and Amazingly Simple Approach to Sock Knitting

With 16 Custom Patterns

Candace Eisner Strick

Strick-ly Socks: A Revolutionary and Amazingly Simple Approach to Sock Knitting
Copyright © 2010 by Candace Eisner Strick
First Printing

Strickwear
P.O. Box 671
Mansfield Centre, CT 06250

Email: Candace@Strickwear.com
Web site: Strickwear.com

Printed in Manitoba, Canada, by Friesens

ISBN: 978-0-615-34511-6

Editor: Nan Newell
Layout: Dolores Schwartz
Photography: F. E. Blefferson
Photo editor: Abraham Lagamoray
Author photo: Kenneth Strick

Also by Candace Eisner Strick

Sweaters From a New England Village
Sweaters From New England Sheep Farms
Beyond Wool
The Quilter's Quick Reference Guide
Little Box of Crocheted Bags
Knit One Stripe Too

Dedication

To my dearest friend and colleague, Judy Pascale:
Chance brought us together; time made us sisters.
Not only have you been a major influence on my
career, but you have also taught me the most
important things about life. We've traveled the
time zones together, and through it all, your
generosity and good spirits have made it fun.
I look forward to the day you will finally break
down and knit socks!

To Kenneth L. Strick, my husband and father of our
three sons: Music brought us together; love made
us one. You are the love of my life. Without your
abiding love and support I could not be.

To my three sons, Nathaniel, Liam, and Noah:
Time is what you are given; passion is how you use
it— you have made me immensely proud.

To my sister, Judith A. Eisner: My worst childhood
nightmare was when I couldn't find you. I share my
earliest and happiest memories with you. "What
goes up the chimney? Smoke. What color is it?
Black, white, gray. May your heart and my heart
never be broke."

And to Nathaniel's beautiful new wife, Jennifer:
I am delighted to welcome you into the Strick family.

To my readers: Knitting, like life, is a journey of discovery. One can be as daring or as cautious as one feels necessary. Jumping into a new sock construction and jumping out of an airplane are daring things for different people. However, the most wonderful thing about knitting is that if you are too daring, and things don't work out, nothing really bad happens.

Acknowledgments

Many people have helped me make this book, which is my seventh. I am extremely indebted to my husband, Ken, who always good-humoredly listened to me either rant about something wrong, or rave about something good. Along with my gratitude for his astounding patience, I consider myself extremely fortunate to have fallen in love with a man whose last name, Strick, means "to knit" in German. Therefore, it occupies a fitting place in the title of this book.

Thanks to Nan Newell, my editor and new-found friend; it was serendipity that you should be the one to pick me up at the Pittsburgh airport. Thank you for your superb editing, advice, and friendship.

Thanks to Cat Bordhi and Margaret Fisher, two self-published authors who generously shared their knowledge of these uncharted waters with me.

Thanks to Ann Feitelson, whose opinions I always trust and value.

Thanks to Myra Finch, who happily sent me the sock yarn she did not want. Who can turn down free yarn?

A bravo and standing ovation to my test knitters—Mary Bishop, Christiane Burkhard, Connie Burmeister, Myra Finch, Jackie Hagen, Selma Kaplan, Pat McMullan, Nan Newell, Gay Robinson, and Cynthia Sanders: You are all so brave, trusting, and totally brilliant!

Thanks to Rosemary "Chappy" Chapman of *Purrfectly Catchy Designs by Chappy* for allowing me to photograph her beautiful sock blockers for this book.

And to the yarn companies who generously supplied me with sock yarn: Plymouth Yarn Company, Universal Yarns, Creatively Dyed Yarn, Ellen's Half-Pint Farm, Miss Babs Hand-Dyed Yarns and Fibers, and Louet Yarn Company.

And a warm and friendly thank-you to all my knitting students, past, present, and future, who trustingly have signed up for my classes throughout the years and laughed at my jokes; may you always merrily knit.

Part 1 - The New Method

Introduction to the New Method · 10

The Formulas · 12

The Nuts and Bolts of Sock Knitting · 13

Casting On · 22
  Foundation row · 24

Sample Socks In BOT and TOT · 25
  BOT toe · 26
  Retrieving live stitches · 27
  Stitch distribution · 28
  Tubular bind-off · 32
  TOT toe · 34

BOT Toe Variations · 36

TOT Toe Variations · 39

The Foot and Gussets · 41

The Heel · 42
  Method #1 Fast decrease · 44
  Method #2 Medium decrease · 45
  Method #3 No decrease · 47
  Heel Options at a Glance · 47

The Cuff · 48

Part 2 - The Patterns

General Information · 53

Happy Feet Basketweave Socks · 54

Short Rib Socks · 56

Wild Iris · 58

Jumpin' Bungee Socks · 60

Mr Congeniality · 62

Ms Congeniality · 64

Raspberry Trifle · 66

Purple Lightning · 68

Smocking Stocking · 70

Howard Johnson · 72

A One-Night Stand with Mochi Plus · 74
   Baby Mochi · 79

Flaming Cables · 76

Spring Chicken · 80

Alien Abduction · 83

Butterfly Silk · 86

Positively Negative · 91

Resources · 94

You probably want to know right away what is different about my new method of knitting socks. If you have always relied on a favorite sock recipe to knit pair after pair, what would make you want to switch to something new? Freedom.

My method will free you from complicated toe-up cast-ons, fussy short-row heels, toes with wrapped stitches, double-wrapped stitches, or hidden wrapped stitches, incessant counting of stitches, and stitch markers to keep your place. And it will free you to do countless variations.

Because my method will have you the master of your sock in no time flat, you are no doubt wondering why something this simple hasn't been published before. I don't know why either, but it's now finally here. Once you try it, you will never look back, and you and your socks will ascend to new levels of creativity.

My new method is all about toes and heels, and it has two basic formulas. The first begins at the base of the toes; the second begins at the tip of the toes. Each method takes you down a different path to toe completion. Both use an easy and superior provisional cast-on; both methods use back-and-forth knitting, not circular, to work the toes and heels.

The soaring popularity of sock knitting, due in part to all the fabulous yarns that have arrived on the scene, has spawned a plethora of books on the subject. A few books offer truly innovative techniques on building a better sock, but others merely plug patterns into the basic sock pattern that I used to knit. My old trusty started at the cuff and worked down to a heel flap; the heel was turned with a series of short rows and decreases. Stitches were then picked up on both sides of the heel flap; those extra stitches were then decreased for the gussets. The foot was worked until about 2 inches before the desired length, and a series of decreases were worked to shape the toe. While I know how to do Kitchener stitch, and don't have a problem with it at all, I hitched the toe stitches together using a three-needle bind-off.

I sometimes plugged in stitch patterns that had a repeat over 56 or 64 stitches, or I adapted my stitch count to use patterns that needed a few stitches more or less. This basic sock fit me perfectly, without a single complaint. So why was I on a quest for a different way? Geometry, especially when applied to knitting, fascinates me. You might say I enjoy looking at things from a different angle. And I am always looking for an easier way to do things.

My heel/toe invention came to me in the effort to make a short-rowed sock without short rows. After examining a basic sock, I could see that the toe, if flattened out and looked at in one dimension, was an hourglass shape—a triangle that is broad at the base, narrowing to the top, and then broadening out again to the original size of the base. A sock heel was exactly the same geometry.

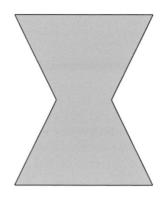

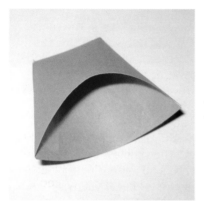

Fold the hourglass horizontally at the waistline, join the diagonal sides, and there you have it.... a perfectly constructed sock toe.

I set to my needles and made a triangle, leaving a neat, chained edge along each side. In order for the sock to become three-dimensional, I would need to pick up and knit along these edges. When I came to the top of the triangle, I started back down the other side, picking up and knitting a stitch in the chain edge at the end of each row. Voilà....I had either a heel or a toe.

I was thrilled and amazed that a toe or heel could be this simple. With each new sock that I knit I discovered many variations within the other parts, all leading to a better sock. All of these ways were simple; they were easy to knit, easy to remember, and totally effective.

I knew I was on to something that other knitters would want to know about. I hope this new method will give you a newfound joy and sense of freedom as you confidently knit socks to fit every foot you know.

You will eventually refer to the formulas as **BOT (BASE OF TOES)** and **TOT (TIP OF TOES)**. These formulas take different approaches to the toe only. All other aspects of both socks, whether worked with a BOT or TOT formula, are exactly the same. Let's take a quick look at both.

BASE OF TOES (BOT) These socks are started at the base of the toes with a provisional cast-on, worked flat with decreases up to the tips of the toes, and then worked down the underside of the toes by working back and forth and picking up one stitch at the end of each row. This method turns the toe. The provisional stitches are then retrieved and the foot is knit in-the-round up to the heel. **The heel is worked the same as the toe.** Gusset increases can be used with this formula, as well as a variety of heel stitch patterns. After the heel is turned, the cuff is worked, and the sock is finished off in a perfectly stretchy and tidy bind-off.

This is a good formula to start with if you already know the number of stitches and size of the needles you will use to make the sock. If you're not sure how long to make the foot of the sock, an existing sock that fits you can be used for a guide.

TIP OF TOES (TOT) This method is worked from the tips of the toes down to the base of the toes. It, too, begins with a provisional cast-on. After the top portion of the toe is worked down to the base of the toes, the stitches are put on hold on a needle while the underside of the toe is worked. The provisional stitches are retrieved and the underside of the toe is then worked down from the tip. Once the toe underside is complete, all stitches are joined and the sock is worked in-the-round until the heel is reached. The heel is constructed the same way as the toe for the BOT formula and the rest of the sock proceeds as for BOT.

This is a good formula to use if you have absolutely no idea how many stitches you are going to use for the sock. Merely cast on 8 or 10 stitches and work the increases until the toe fits. This is also a good formula to use if you are using self-striping yarn and wish to have the stripe sequence, from the tips of the toes up to the bind-off, go in the same direction. (BOT would not work in this case, as the pattern on the toe would be going in one direction towards the tips of the toes, then would be reversed when working the instep stitches up to the top of the cuff.)

These socks, whether BOT or TOT, will fit any foot and any leg. The simplest sock pattern in this book involves no increasing or decreasing for a gusset. But if you wish, you can add increases for a gusset to fit a person with a higher instep, or to just give a little extra ease over the ankle area. If you like socks with the traditional slipped-stitch heel pattern, you can do that also. You can even make a sock that is totally reversible. Why would you want a reversible sock? I don't really know, except that the idea is very cool.

Either method—BOT or TOT—involves a minimum of stitch counting. You won't need stitch markers and you won't have to pay constant attention to a lengthy or complicated pattern or chart. You will be able to pick up your project at a moment's notice without wondering where you left off, or put it down without fear of losing your place.

I highly suggest knitting a sample BOT or TOT sock in stockinette stitch first. Once you have mastered the basic techniques, you can experiment with all sorts of variations or you can have fun with one of the 16 patterns for socks included in this book.

Strick-ly Socks

SOCK TERMINOLOGY

Base of toe: This is the part of the foot where your toes attach to the foot proper. It is the opposite of the term "tip of toe," where your toenails reside.

Tip of toe: This is the top part of the toe, or what you would be standing on if you were a ballerina. It is the opposite of the term "base of toe."

Topside of toe: This is the part of the sock that covers the portion of the toes you can see when looking down.

Underside of toe: This is the part of the sock that covers the backside of your toes, or the part that touches the floor when you walk. The underside of the toe is always worked from the tip of the toe to the base of the toe.

Instep: This is the top of your foot. It never makes contact with the ground.

Sole: This is the part of your foot that walks on the ground. The sole merges into the underside of the heel.

Underside of Heel: This is the part you walk on. The underside of the heel merges into the outside of the heel.

Outside of Heel: This is the part that covers the backside of your heel. If you wear clogs, this back part of your heel will not rub against anything, as it does when you wear shoes.

Cuff: This is the entire portion of the sock that starts at the completion of the heel. It covers the lower leg and ends with the bind-off.

Front cuff: This is the portion of the cuff that continues from the instep stitches.

Back cuff: This is the portion that continues from the sole and then the heel stitches.

PATTERN ABBREVIATIONS

Note: Abbreviations marked with an asterisk are fully explained in the techniques section immediately following.

beg	begin, beginning
BO	bind off
*CE	chain edge
cn	cable needle
CO	cast on
cont	continue
dec(s)	decrease(s), decreasing
dpn(s)	double-pointed needle(s)
est	established
foll	following
GS	garter stitch
inc(s)	increase(s), increasing
K	knit
*K1tbl	knit 1 stitch through back loop
*Kfb	knit front and back
*K2tog	knit 2 stitches together
LH	left-hand
*M1L	make 1 knit stitch slanting left
*M1R	make 1 knit stitch slanting right
*M1P	make 1 purl stitch
P	purl
*P1tbl	purl 1 stitch through back loop
patt	pattern
pu	pick up
rem	remaining, remainder
rep	repeat
RH	right-hand
rnd(s)	round(s)
RS	right side
*ssk	slip 1 stitch knitwise, slip 1 stitch knitwise, insert left-hand needle through the fronts of these two stitches and knit them together
stock st	stockinette stitch
st(s)	stitch(es)
tog	together
wyib	with yarn in back
wyif	with yarn in front
WS	wrong side
*YO	yarnover

Strick-ly Socks

TECHNIQUES - CHAIN EDGE (CE) IN STOCKINETTE STITCH

Knit rows (RS): With yarn in back slip first stitch purlwise.

Finished chain edge shown from right side.

Purl rows (WS): With yarn in front slip first stitch purlwise.

Finished chain edge shown from wrong side.

TECHNIQUES - CHAIN EDGE (CE) IN GARTER STITCH

With yarn in front slip first stitch purlwise.

Return yarn to back of work by putting it between the needles.

Finished chain edge shown in garter stitch.

TECHNIQUES - INCREASES

Make 1 Left (M1L)

With left-hand needle pick up horizontal thread between two stitches from front to back.

Knit into the back of this loop (makes a left-leaning increase).

Make 1 Right (M1R)

With left-hand needle pick up horizontal thread between two stitches from back to front.

Knit into the front of this loop (makes a right-leaning increase).

Knit Front and Back (Kfb)

Knit into the front of the stitch.

Then knit into the back.

Yarnover (YO)

 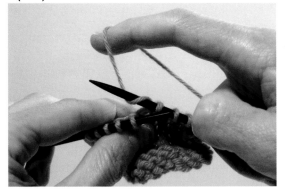

Place yarn from front to back over right-hand needle.

(Exception: For the TOT toe, there is a yarnover that is specified as placing the yarn from back to front over the right-hand needle.)

Make 1 Purl (M1P)

With left-hand needle pick up horizontal thread between two stitches from front to back.

Purl into the back of this loop.

Strick-ly Socks

TECHNIQUES - DECREASES

Knit 2 together (K2tog)

Insert left-hand needle into the fronts of the
two stitches and knit them together (makes
a right-leaning decrease).

Slip slip knit (SSK)

Slip 1 stitch knitwise, slip 1 stitch knitwise.

Insert left-hand needle into the fronts of
these 2 stitches and knit them together
(makes a left-leaning decrease).

Knit though back loop (Ktbl)

Insert needle into back of stitch from right to left, knit.

Purl through back loop (Ptbl)

Insert right-hand needle into the back of the stitch from left to right, purl.

YARN

Generally, sock-weight yarn comes in either 50-gram skeins or 100-gram skeins. If using 50-gram skeins, you will need 2 skeins to make an adult pair of socks, or about 456 yards/440 meters. If using a 100-gram skein and the yardage for that particular skein has about 456 yards/440 meters, then one skein will make an adult pair of socks.

Sock-weight yarn generally is anywhere from 75% to 80% wool, with the remaining percentage being nylon. Some sock yarn is 100% wool or superwash wool. When using yarn that does not have nylon content, I like to use reinforcing yarn on my heels. It is available to purchase in a wide variety of colors, or sometimes it comes along with the skein of sock yarn. Simply carry the strand of reinforcing yarn along with the regular yarn, knitting both together.

NEEDLES

If using sock-weight yarn, generally any size needle from 0-2 (2 mm-2.75 mm) works well, depending on how you knit. Always check your gauge.

SOCK SIZE

Yes, size does matter. For a sock to be functional, it must fit properly. If it is too big, you will end up folding and bunching it in order to get your shoe on, and then it will be quite uncomfortable. If too small, well....it just won't go on your foot.

Every sock should have what is called in the industry "negative ease." That is, the finished product should be smaller than your foot, and the magic ratio for this is about 10%. In other words, if your bare foot measures 8" around the widest part (see photo) and your gauge is 9 sts = 1 inch, then your total number of stitches should be 72 minus 10%, or 64.8 sts. You can either round up or down for the total number. Foot length is easily adaptable by working extra rounds. The ankle area and cuff are both easily adaptable for special needs (see page 47).

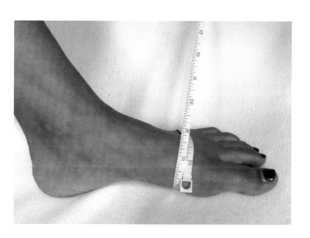

Both toe methods begin with a provisional cast-on. While I have always liked to use the Channel Island cast-on as a permanent cast-on, I discovered that it also makes an incredibly good provisional cast-on. When done with two yarns of different colors, the stitches that need to be picked up are easy to see, easy to pick up, and you wind up with the same number of stitches that were originally cast on. This cast-on always yields an even number of stitches.

I highly advise practicing this cast-on using a thicker-than-sock-weight yarn, and large needles. If you wish to practice a TOT toe, cast on 8 stitches. For a BOT toe, cast on 32 stitches. Continue working the toe for this practice, right through to retrieving the live stitches. After a successful practice toe, you should be ready to start on a real sock!

CHANNEL ISLAND CAST-ON

The Channel Island cast-on will be used here as a provisional cast-on, which means that the waste yarn used will be pulled out to yield live stitches. The yarn is tensioned in the left hand; the needle is held in the right hand.

You will need 2 strands of yarn: one is the waste yarn, the other is the sock yarn. For the waste yarn, use 1 strand of a somewhat heavier weight yarn than the sock yarn, and in a very contrasting color to the sock yarn. You will need about 1 yard. The second strand is the sock yarn; use it as it comes from the ball (do not cut a separate length) and leave a tail of about 6 inches.

Place a slipknot on the needle with both strands of yarn held together. **The slipknot does not count as a stitch.** Tension the single strand of sock yarn as you would normally do for knitting or crocheting.

The strand of sock yarn goes over the left forefinger; the other strand is the waste yarn that will be picked out later on and discarded. The empty needle is held in the right hand.

1. Wrap the strand of waste yarn around the left thumb counterclockwise twice. If you have a hard time visualizing counterclockwise, think of it this way: When the yarn is draped between your thumb and forefinger going from back to front, there is only one direction that you can wrap it around your thumb.

2. Drape the strand of sock yarn over the needle as if doing a yarnover (front to back over right-hand needle).

3. Insert the needle under all the waste strand loops on thumb from bottom to top.

4. Come over the top of the strand of sock yarn and use it to pull a stitch through the thumb strands.

5. Tighten the stitch on the needle by gently pulling on the strand of waste yarn. Each sequence of steps 1 through 5 yields 2 stitches on the needle. The first stitch looks like a yarn-over loop on the needle; the second stitch looks like a real stitch, and there is a bead of provisional (i.e., waste) yarn under it.

6. Repeat steps 1 through 5 until the correct number of stitches is on the needle. **Remember that the slipknot does not count as a stitch.**

FOUNDATION ROW

Before you can actually start working the sock, a foundation row must first be worked. The number of stitches on your needle depends on whether you have decided to work the BOT toe or the TOT toe.

The foundation row is worked using the sock yarn. It is a wrong-side row that can be worked in stockinette or garter stitch. In order for this cast-on to yield the correct number of live stitches, it is imperative that this first row be worked correctly.

Foundation Row for Stockinette Stitch Toe

1. Purl through the back loop of the first stitch. Transfer that stitch purlwise back to the left-hand needle and purl it again in regular position (not through the back loop).

2. Purl across the row to the last stitch.

3. Purl through the back loop of the last stitch. Transfer the last stitch back to the left-hand needle and purl it again in regular position (not through the back).

4. Drop the slipknot off the needle. Do not weave in the tail of sock yarn, as it will be used later to work one stitch. Begin working the first right-side row of the sock toe.

Foundation Row for Garter Stitch Toe

1. Purl through the back loop of the first stitch. Transfer that stitch purlwise back to the left-hand needle and knit it.

2. Knit across the row to the last stitch. Purl through the back loop of the last stitch. Transfer the last stitch back to the left-hand needle and knit it.

3. Drop the slipknot off the needle. Do not weave in the tail of sock yarn, as it will be used later to work one stitch.

4. Begin working the first right-side row of the sock toe for either BOT or TOT.

Strick-ly Socks

Sample Socks in BOT and TOT

If you have already mastered the cast-on, you may feel confident enough to begin a real sock. This sample sock is the most simple and basic; it is all stockinette stitch in one color, there are no gussets, and the heel is worked on 50% of the total number of stitches. Once you have mastered the general plan of my new sock, you can then go on to try some or all of the variations that are later explained.

I suggest you make one sock using the BOT method, and make the mate using the TOT method. This way, you will have a completed pair of socks that demonstrates your mastery of both methods.

For this sample BOT sock there are a total of 64 stitches. (The simplicity of the formula, however, allows it to work on any number of stitches. While a 64-stitch sock worked in sock-weight yarn will fit a medium adult foot, the sock can also be worked on any other number of stitches by following the general directions.) The numbers in the parentheses relate to the 64-stitch sock.

The directions are written for using double-pointed needles. If you wish, you may substitute two circulars or one long circular needle. For complete directions using methods other than double-pointed needles, there are many excellent books available, as well as numerous tutorials on the Internet.

YARN
Sock-weight yarn
3.5 oz; 100 gms/456 yards; 440 m

NEEDLES
One set double-pointed size 0 (2.0 mm) or size needed to obtain gauge

GAUGE   9 sts = 1" in stock st

SIZE   64 sts = Adult Medium

PATTERN STITCH
Stockinette Stitch
Back-and-forth: Knit the right-side rows, purl the wrong-side rows.
In-the-round: Knit every round.

BOT TOE

The cast-on, topside, and underside of the toe are worked back-and-forth using 2 double-pointed needles.

Channel Island CO one-half the total number of stitches for the sock (32). Work the foundation row as specified for stockinette stitch, then begin the topside of the toe.

Topside BOT Toe in Stockinette Stitch

The first row is a right-side row. The first stitch of each row makes a chain edge (CE).

Row 1: With yarn in back, slip stitch purlwise (CE), knit 2, ssk, knit to last 5 stitches, knit 2 together, knit 3.
Row 2: With yarn in front, slip stitch purlwise (CE), purl to end of row.

Repeat rows 1 and 2 until desired number of stitches remain (8), ending with a completed row 2. Continue by working the underside toe in stockinette stitch.

When working stockinette stitch, work the CE as follows:
Right-Side Rows: With yarn in back, slip stitch purlwise.
Wrong-Side Rows: With yarn in front, slip stitch purlwise.
Think of it as always slipping the first stitch purlwise with the yarn in the working position.

Underside BOT Toe in Stockinette Stitch

Note: Remember to stop working chain edges for this portion of toe.
Row 1 (RS): Knit across the stitches, pick up and knit 1 st in first chain edge [yarn is in back, needle goes into chain from front (right side of work) to back (wrong side of work); wrap yarn and knit up a stitch]—(9).

Row 2: With WS facing, purl across row, working the first stitch of the row very firmly. Pick up and purl 1 st in first chain edge [yarn is in front, needle goes into chain from back (right side of work) to front (wrong side of work); wrap yarn and purl up a stitch]—(10).

Strick-ly Socks

Row 3: Knit across sts, knitting the first stitch very firmly. Pick up and knit into next chain—(11).
Row 4: Purl across sts, working the first stitch very firmly. Pick up and purl into next chain—(12).

Repeat rows 3 and 4 until there is 1 less stitch (31) than the original cast-on (32).

This portion of the sock will always end with a completed RS row. Do not turn work. At this point it is advisable to distribute the stitches of the toe underside onto two needles. These stitches will soon be referred to as the sole stitches. Needle #1 will have one less stitch than needle #2 (i.e., needle #1: 15 sts, needle #2: 16 sts). Continue with retrieving the live stitches.

RETRIEVING THE LIVE STITCHES

It is now time to retrieve the stitches for the instep (needle #3).
When you look at the right side of the sock you will see individual stitches worked in sock yarn that have the waste yarn running right through them. There will be a complete stitch in every bead of the waste yarn. Run an empty needle through the sock yarn stitches that have the provisional waste yarn going through the middle of them.

Take a pointy pair of scissors and cut through each of the Channel Island cast-on provisional beads, being very careful not to cut the sock yarn. Carefully pull out the small sections of the provisional yarn. I sometimes use a seam ripper as a safety measure to cut the waste yarn between the stitches, because it means I won't be doing any cutting near the permanent stitches. You may also use a spare needle to pick out the knot of the waste yarn bead.

DISTRIBUTING STITCHES ONTO NEEDLES

You will be using three needles to hold the stitches and one more needle to work the stitches. The instep stitches are all held on one needle, #3. The sole stitches are divided onto two needles, #1 and #2. All rounds begin and end after the instep stitches are worked on needle #3. For example, the round begins with needle #1, which holds one-half of the sole stitches. Needle #2 holds the second half of the sole stitches. Needle #3 holds the instep stitches.

If you wish to use 4 double-pointed needles and work the stitches with the fifth needle, divide sole stitches as for 3 needles, but divide the instep stitches onto two needles, #3 and #4. You will then have 4 needles each holding the same number of stitches. All rounds still begin and end after the instep stitches are worked.

If you are using two circular needles, place all the sole stitches onto needle #1; place all the instep stitches onto needle #2. All rounds still begin and end after the instep stitches are worked.

If you are using the magic loop method, distribute as for two circulars.

The sole stitches are divided onto needles #1 and #2. The instep stitches are on needle #3.

Strick-ly Socks

Uniting the BOT underside with instep stitches

The next stitches (32) to be worked are the instep stitches on needle #3 which were retrieved from the provisional cast-on. The first two stitches from the provisional cast-on will be somewhat twisted around each other. Knit through the back loop of the first stitch. Knit through the back of the next two stitches. Now every other stitch on the needle will be mounted with the left leg presenting. Knit through the backs of these left-leg stitches and through the fronts of the conventionally mounted right-leg stitches. After this first round all the stitches will then be in the correct orientation. All rounds begin and end after the instep stitches on needle #3.

Stitch as it appears off the needle.
Right side of loop is right leg.
Left side of loop is left leg.

Left leg presenting

Right leg presenting

The next round requires one more stitch to be picked up and knit in the chain edge. This stitch belongs on needle #1. Begin the round by picking up and knitting this stitch with the tail of the yarn that was left from the cast-on. Transfer it to needle #1. Tighten the tail from the wrong side, and this stitch should now be perfect. You may weave in this tail of yarn now, as it won't be used again. Needle #1 has one-half of the sole sts, needle #2 has the other half of the sole sts, and needle #3 has all of the instep sts. Rounds begin and end after instep stitches on needle #3.
(needle #1: 16; needle #2: 16; needle #3: 32)

Foot

Work the foot in stockinette stitch until it is time to start the heel. You may try your sock on your foot to determine where to start the heel. Unless you are working on two circulars, you will have to distribute the instep stitches onto two needles, which will allow you to try the sock on to get a true fit. When the sock reaches the indentation of the inside foot it is time to start the heel.

If this is difficult to gauge, you can also use an existing sock as a template. If the existing sock has been knit with a traditional heel flap and gusset, start the heel on your sock when the foot reaches the junction of the heel flap and gusset beginning. You can easily mark your foot by putting a ballpoint pen through the sock on your foot to make a small mark (X marks the spot in the photo). Now when you try on your sock in progress you know exactly where to start working the heel.

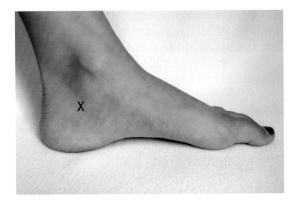

Basic Heel

Work the heel back and forth on 2 double-pointed needles the same way as the BOT toe, except that now there is no need for any provisional stitches. Place the heel stitches (32) onto one needle and divide the instep stitches onto 2 needles. The basic heel is worked on 50% of the total stitches, which is 100% of the sole stitches.

Basic Heel Underside: Knit the first stitch on the needle. Transfer it back to the left-hand needle. Work the **Topside BOT Toe in Stockinette Stitch** until there are 8 sts.

Basic Heel Outside: Work the **Underside BOT Toe** by turning and picking up for stockinette stitch until there is one stitch left to be picked up. Work this stitch using the regular working yarn (for the toe, this last stitch was worked using the tail of the yarn).

Strick-ly Socks

Cuff

Work the cuff in stockinette stitch until desired length. If you're not sure about how long to make the cuff, use this handy-dandy ratio which requires no math or tape measure. Fold the sole of the sock until the heel flattens out. If the cuff can fold back and be the same length as the foot, the proportions will be exactly right. In other words, if the cuff is the same length as the sole, the sock will be in the correct proportions. Of course, if you want a shorter cuff, just disregard this tip and make it the length you wish. Remember, however, that most socks end with a ribbing.

To make the ribbing, repeat the following row until ribbing is the desired length, ending with a completed round at the end of the instep stitches on needle #3:

Knit 1, purl 1, repeat between *s.

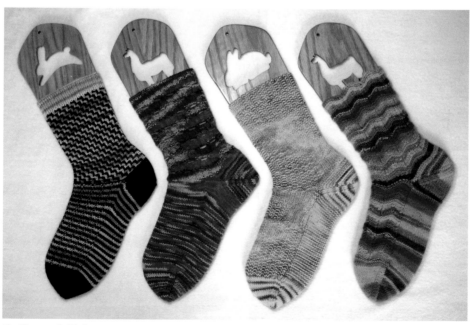

Cuff possibilities. (Left to right)
Alien Abduction page 83, Smocking Stocking page 70, Wild Iris page 58, Raspberry Trifle page 66.

Tubular Bind-Off for K1, P1 Ribbing

Now that your fantastic sock is almost complete, you will want to make sure you will be able to get it on your foot. Sometimes the standard bind-off is just too tight, and the very end of your wonderful experience ends in disappointment—I am putting this very mildly! The tubular bind-off leaves a beautifully clean and stretchy ending to your perfect sock.

For demonstration purposes only, the bind-off yarn is shown in a different color.

Thread a tail of yarn about 3 times the circumference of the sock top through a tapestry needle. Hold work with right side facing.

Step 1: Bring the tapestry needle from back to front between the first 2 stitches.

Step 2: Insert the tapestry needle knitwise through the second stitch (which is a purl stitch) and draw to back of work. (Knit on)

Step 3: Bring the tapestry needle to front by going under the knitting needle and insert the tapestry needle knitwise through first stitch (which is a knit stitch) and drop that stitch from the knitting needle. (Knit off)

Strick-ly Socks

Step 4: Insert the tapestry needle purlwise through second stitch on the knitting needle (which is a knit stitch) and draw through. (Purl on)

Step 5: Insert the tapestry needle purlwise through first stitch on the knitting needle (which is a purl stitch) and drop that stitch from the knitting needle and draw through. (Purl Off)

One completed bound-off stitch

Repeat steps 1-5. When there is one stitch remaining insert the tapestry needle knitwise through the stitch and drop it off the knitting needle. Fasten tail by going through the middle of the first bound-off stitch; work a duplicate stitch in that stitch, then weave the tail in on the wrong-side.

Completed sock bind-off

Voilà....there is your sock. Now that you know the basic construction for the BOT Toe sock, why not make the mate by trying the TOT Toe? After that, you will be familiar with both methods.

THE TOT TOE

For this sample TOT sock there are a total of 64 stitches; the sock will be worked in stockinette stitch. General directions are given, as well as specific numbers for the sample sock, which will be in parentheses. The directions are written for using double-pointed needles. Stitch distribution is the same as the BOT method.

Yarn requirements and materials are the same as for BOT. Like the BOT sock, the simplicity of this formula allows it to work with any number of stitches.

The cast-on, topside, and underside of the toe are worked back and forth on 2 double-pointed needles.

Channel Island CO 8 stitches. Work the foundation row for stockinette stitch. The topside of the toe is worked first. It starts at the tip of the toes and works down to the base of the toes.

Strick-ly Socks

Topside of TOT Toe in Stockinette Stitch

The first stitch of each row makes a chain edge (CE).
Begin increasing, starting with a right-side row.

Row 1 (RS): With yarn in back, slip stitch purlwise (CE), knit 2, yarn over needle back to front (1 st increased), knit to last 3 stitches, yarnover needle front to back (1 st increased), knit 3.

Row 2 (WS): With yarn in front, slip stitch purlwise (CE), p2, purl through the back loop of the yarn-over from the previous row, purl to 4 stitches before end, purl the yarnover from the previous row, p3.

Repeat rows 1 and 2 until there are one-half (32) the total number of stitches desired for sock (64), ending with a completed row 2. This needle and these stitches will later be referred to as the instep stitches (needle #3). Do not break yarn. Begin working the underside of the toe.
Note: You may find it easier to temporarily distribute the instep stitches onto 2 needles while you are nearing the completion of the toe underside. After completion, place all the instep stitches back onto one needle.

Underside TOT Toe in Stockinette Stitch

With the right side facing, retrieve the stitches (8) from the provisional cast-on as for BOT. Use the other end of yarn, or a new ball of yarn for the toe underside. The first pick-up row is a right-side row. Work the TOT underside the same as the Underside BOT Toe in stockinette stitch until there is 1 less stitch than one-half the total number (31). This will be the end of a right-side row. Do not turn work.

Uniting TOT underside with the instep stitches

Break the yarn used for the underside of the toe. Picking up the original yarn that was left at the beginning of needle #3, knit across the instep stitches. Pick up and knit the last stitch in the chain edge and place it on needle #1. For the sole there is now one-half the total number of stitches for the sock (32) distributed equally onto 2 needles (16 on each needle), and one-half the total number of stitches for the instep stitches on one needle (32).
(Needle #1: 16; needle #2: 16; needle #3: 32)
Work remainder of sock as for sample BOT sock.

Now that you have mastered the basic formula for either the BOT or TOT sock—or both, there are many unique things you can do to customize your basic sock so they fit different feet more efficiently. These variations are all explained in the next two chapters.

Number of Stitches

While the basic formula of BOT adapts to any number of stitches, anything less than a total of 24 stitches would get unwieldy.

If working with an odd number, cast on 2 more stitches than the desired number. Work the toe with the even number, then knit the first two stitches together on the first row of the instep stitches to yield an odd number.

If a less pointed toe is desired, work until 10 or 12 stitches remain.

If a more pointed toe is desired, or a very small-sized sock is being worked, or thicker yarn is being used, work until there are 6 stitches. For 6 stitch toe work until 8 stitches remain, then work the following 2 rows:

Row 1: CE for either garter stitch or stockinette stitch, knit 1, ssk, knit 2 together, knit 2.
Row 2: CE for either garter stitch or stockinette stitch, knit or purl to end of row.

The foot always begins with an even number of sole stitches. If an odd number of sole stitches is required to work a particular heel, an increase can be made on any round anywhere within the foot.

Garter stitch toe. Ms Congeniality, page 64

Topside BOT Toe in Garter Stitch

The first row is a right-side row. The first stitch of each row makes a chain edge (CE). A garter stitch toe is totally reversible.

Row 1: With yarn in front, slip stitch purlwise, return yarn to the back of the work by placing it between the needles (CE), knit 2, ssk, knit to last 5 stitches, knit 2 together, knit 3.
Row 2: With yarn in front, slip stitch purlwise, return yarn to the back of the work by placing it between the needles (CE), knit to end of row.

Repeat rows 1 and 2 until desired number of stitches remains (8), ending with a completed row 2. Continue by working the underside toe for chosen pattern stitch.

Underside BOT Toe in Garter Stitch (makes toe reversible)

Note: Remember to stop working chain edges for this portion of toe.

Row 1 (RS): Knit across the stitches, pick up and knit 1 st in first chain edge [yarn is in back, needle goes into chain from front (right side of work) to back (wrong side of the work); wrap yarn and knit up a stitch]—(9).
Row 2: With WS facing, knit across row, working the first stitch of the row very firmly. Pick up and knit 1 st in first chain edge [yarn is in back, needle goes into chain from front (wrong side of the work) to back (right side of the work); wrap yarn and knit up a stitch]—(10).

Repeat rows 1 and 2 until there is 1 less stitch than the original cast-on. This portion of the sock will always end with a completed RS row. Do not turn work. Continue as for basic sock.

Strick-ly Socks

Other patterns for BOT toe

You can work in any pattern that fits into the BOT toe. Because the toe begins with the most number of stitches and decreases up to the top, patterns with a triangular motif fit into the toe nicely. These patterns can be easily plotted out on graph paper using the template below.

Because the toe is worked back-and-forth, you can easily work a two-color charted pattern, which would look very cool when wearing the socks with sandals.

Positively Negative, page 91

Toe

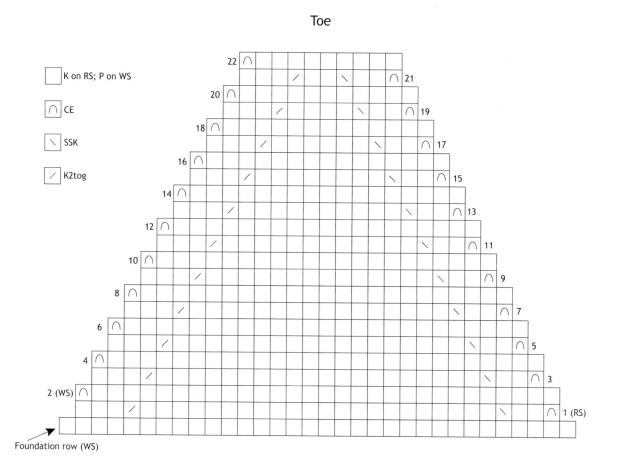

Foundation row (WS)

Dealing with self-striping yarn or different colors

If you are working with a self-striping yarn and wish the stripes to continue in the same sequence from the tip of the toe up through the instep and cuff, begin the BOT using the other end of the ball of yarn. Once the toe is completed, begin the foot with the opposite end of yarn.

If you have decided to work the toe with yarn of a different color from that of the foot of the sock, break the toe yarn once all the stitches have been picked up and continue with the new color.

Chain Edge (CE)

When working garter stitch, work the CE as follows:
With yarn in front, slip stitch purlwise, return yarn to back of work by placing it between the needles.

When working stockinette stitch, work the CE as follows:
Right-Side Rows: With yarn in back, slip stitch purlwise.
Wrong-Side Rows: With yarn in front, slip stitch purlwise.

Think of it as always slipping the first stitch purlwise with the yarn in the working position.

Strick-ly Socks

Dealing with self-striping yarn or different colors

This toe allows the stripe sequence to
continue uninterrupted from the tip of the toe
up to the cuff. If you work the foot without
any gussets, and work the heel using the other
end of the skein, the sock will have a perfect
stripe sequence.

Raspberry Trifle, page 66

If you have decided to work the toe with a
different color yarn than the foot of the
sock, break the toe yarn once all the
stitches have been picked up and continue
with the new color.

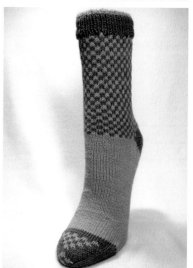

Positively Negative, page 91

Number of Stitches

If the sock requires an odd number of stitches
beginning right at the toe, work 2 stitches
together in the middle of the first right-side
row as follows: CE, k2, k2together, k3.

I like to start my toe with either 8 or 10
stitches, but for a smaller sock or a sock knit
from thicker yarn, you could start the toe
with 6 stitches. In this case, work the first
increase row for either stockinette stitch or
garter stitch, working the CE appropriately
for the stitch, as follows:

First increase row (RS): CE, k2, inc 1, inc 1, k3.

The foot always begins with an even number
of sole stitches.

If an odd number of sole stitches is required
to work a particular heel, an increase can be
made on any round anywhere within the foot.

Stitch Patterns

Topside of TOT Toe in Garter Stitch

Row 1: With yarn in front, slip stitch purlwise, return yarn to the back of work by placing it between the needles (CE), knit 2, yarnover (1 stitch increased), knit to last 3 stitches, yarnover (1 stitch increased), k3.

Row 2: With yarn in front, slip stitch purlwise, return yarn to back of work by placing it between the needles (CE), knit 2, knit through back loop of yarnover from previous row, knit to 4 stitches before end of row, knit through back loop of yarnover from the previous row, knit 3.

Repeat rows 1 and 2 until there are one-half the total number of stitches desired for sock, ending with a completed Row 2. This needle and these stitches will later be referred to as the instep stitches (needle #3). Do not break yarn. Begin working the underside of the toe with a new end of yarn. *Note: You may find it easier to temporarily distribute the instep stitches onto 2 needles while you are nearing the completion of the toe underside. After completion, place all the instep stitches back onto one needle.*

Underside of TOT Toe in Garter Stitch
Work as for BOT underside in garter stitch.

Other patterns for TOT toe
You can work in any pattern that fits into the TOT toe. Because the toe begins with the least number of stitches and increases to the base, patterns that are triangular shaped, or broaden out from a small number of stitches to a larger number of stitches fit into the toe nicely. Here is a generic graph for a TOT toe starting with 10 stitches. Feel free to copy the graph and experiment with charting designs.

Toe

Chart legend:

- ∩ CE
- ○ YO (Purl into back on WS)
- ⊖ YO back to front (Purl into front on WS)
- ☐ K on RS; P on WS

Rows (right to left / bottom to top as labeled): Foundation row (WS), 1 (RS), 2 (WS), 3, 4, 5, 6, 7, 8, 9, 10, 11, 12, 13, 14, 15, 16, 17, 18, 19, 20, 21, 22

Now that your toe in either BOT or TOT is completed, the remainder of the sock is worked the same regardless of the toe method. The instep stitches are on needle #3 and the sole stitches are on needles #1 and #2.

The foot always begins with an even number of sole stitches. (If an odd number of sole stitches is required to work a particular heel, an increase can be made anywhere within working the sole.) The sole stitches are almost always worked in stockinette stitch. There are a few exceptions to this, as in the totally reversible socks of Mr and Ms Congeniality (See page 62, 64).

The instep stitches can be worked in any pattern, as long as the stitch multiple works with the number of stitches on the instep. The instep pattern can be continued up through the front cuff, or the front and back cuff can be united into one continuous pattern.

To gusset or not to gusset

Traditionally, knit socks incorporate gusset stitches into the sock. This allows a little extra room to accommodate the instep of the foot. If you decide on no gussets, you still may work the heel on a larger percentage of stitches for a little extra room. This is explained in the next chapter, which is devoted to heels.

Gussets

In either BOT or TOT, gussets can begin shortly before the heel is started. Once a small portion of the foot has been knit, an accurate row gauge can be taken to determine when to start the gussets. Or you may use an existing sock as a template.

For most adult feet, a sock worked in sock-weight yarn with 14 or 16 extra stitches for the gusset is about standard. For a smaller-sized sock, 12 or 10 extra stitches would be

sufficient. One stitch is increased on each side of the sole stitches every other round to yield an increase of 2 stitches every other round. For an extra 14 stitches, the gusset is started 14 rounds before the heel is started; for an extra 16 stitches the gusset is started 16 rounds before the heel is started. Increasing is done every other round on the sole stitches by working the following 2 rounds:

Rnd 1 (needle #1 of sole stitches): K1, M1L, knit to end of needle. Knit the stitches of needle #2 until 1 stitch remains, M1R, knit last stitch. Work instep stitches.

Rnd 2: Work all stitches on all needles. Repeat these two rounds until desired sock size is reached. Once these two rounds have been completed, you will need to decide on the type of heel you want.

Remember that there are now extra sole stitches; one-half of them are at the beginning of needle #1; the other half are at the end of needle #2. These extra stitches will now have to be whittled down (or maybe not!). There are five ways this can be done, all explained in the next chapter.

When using self-striping yarn, incorporating gussets will disturb the width of the stripes as each round will become a little longer. If this bothers you, try working the heel on 60% of the stitches to give a little extra room. If you use the other end of the skein, or a different yarn for the heel, the stripes will stay in perfect harmony.

While all parts of a sock are important, the heel is critical to a good fit. There are many options for working the heel, and each has its own unique properties for providing a better fit.

The heel and the toe are exactly the same, but just reside in different places on the sock. The undersides of all heels are worked the same as the Topside BOT Toe, and outsides of all heel are worked the same as the Underside BOT Toe (see page 26).

The heel can be worked in a variety of stitches. I almost always work the underside in stockinette stitch, which is smooth and comfortable to stand on. The outside can be worked in stockinette or garter stitch (see page 36 for garter stitch), or the Slip-Stitch Heel pattern (see page 43).

You may use reinforcing thread in any part of your heel. Because I tend to wear my socks only with clogs or sandals, the outside heel does not get any abrasion, so I reinforce only the underside portion.

Working the basic heel on more than 50% of the stitches

A heel worked on 50% of the stitches will fit most average feet. However, the more stitches the heel is worked on, the wider and deeper it becomes. In a sock that has been knit without gussets, working the heel on 60% of the stitches is an easy way to add a little more room in the instep. To provide a better fit for a person with a broad heel, you may work the underside heel until a larger number of stitches remain (9, 11, or 13) before beginning the heel outside.

For a 64-stitch sock, 60% of the stitches is 38 stitches. If your pattern requires an odd number of stitches (for example, if the outside of the heel is to be worked in a Slip-Stitch Heel pattern), you would have already worked an increase somewhere in the sole. In this case, the heel would be worked on 39 stitches.

Work the last round before the heel until 3 stitches remain on the instep needle. Take these 3 stitches and transfer them to the beginning of needle #1; take 3 stitches from the other end of the instep stitches and transfer them to the end of the needle #2. Work as for basic heel on 38 or 39 stitches in stitch pattern of your choice. When the heel has been completed, place the 3 extra stitches from each end of the heel needle back to each end of the instep needle.

Heel without gussets - 60%
Heel underside in stockinette stitch
Heel outside in garter stitch

Wild Iris, page 58

Working the Slip-Stitch Heel pattern on the outside heel

This pattern requires an odd number of stitches so that it will be symmetrical. This is accomplished by increasing 1 stitch somewhere in the sole. Work the underside of the heel in desired stitch pattern.

Begin the outside of the heel with 7, 9, 11, or 13 stitches. It is worked in the same manner as the basic heel outside, but in the following stitch pattern:

Slip-Stitch Heel pattern

Row 1: *Knit 1, with yarn in back slip 1 stitch purlwise*, repeat between *s to end of row, pick up one stitch knitwise in chain edge.

Row 2: Purl across all stitches, pick up 1 stitch purlwise in chain edge.

Row 3: Work as row 1, but begin row with slip 1.

Row 4: Work as row 2.

Continue working in above manner, alternating working the first stitch of the row with what was worked on the previous right-side row. In other words, continue the *slip 1, k1* pattern for Row 1 throughout, working the extra stitches into established pattern. All wrong-side rows are worked as for row 2.

Work the heel until all stitches have been picked up. If you wish this slip-stitch portion to be a little higher, you can work a few more rows of the pattern into the cuff, as long as you're not interfering with any stitch pattern. If you choose to do this, remember that you are now working in the round, so every other row will be knit.

Hint: If you lose your place in the Slip-Stitch Heel pattern, pay attention to each WS row as you purl it. It is easy to see which stitches are slipped and which are purled. When nearing the end of the WS row, remember whether the last stitch was a slip stitch or a worked stitch.

When the basic heel has been completed, readjust the stitches if necessary (i.e., if the heel was worked with more than 50% of the stitches) to the proper positions on the needles. You are now ready to proceed with the cuff portion of the sock (See page 48).

Heel worked in Slip-Stitch pattern.
Purple Lightning, page 68

Heels for socks with gussets

If gussets have been worked, the extra stitches have to be dealt with. For most socks, the extra stitches need to be decreased down to the original number. This can be done in a number of different ways, depending upon individual foot and/or leg size—Fast, Medium, Slow or NO!

METHOD #1 — THE FAST DECREASE
50% OF HEEL STITCHES PLUS GUSSET STITCHES

This method accomplishes the decreases while working the underside of the heel. It is good for providing a little extra room in the instep while keeping the ankle and cuff portion of the sock in the original stitch count. This keeps any stitch patterns in the cuff intact.

All of the heel stitches plus the extra gusset stitches should now be on needles #1 and #2. Remember to work the appropriate CE for either stockinette stitch or garter stitch. Work the following 2 rows for as many times as you worked the 2 rows of gusset increases. Two stitches are decreased on each side of the heel on every RS row until the extra stitches are eliminated.

Row 1: CE, k2, ssk, ssk, knit to last 7 stitches, k2tog, k2tog, k3 — (4 sts dec).
Row 2: CE, purl for stockinette stitch, knit for garter stitch.

After all the extra gusset stitches are decreased, continue working as for basic heel (1 stitch decreased on each side every other row).

Method #1 - The Fast Decrease
Ms Congeniality, page 64

If working with self-striping yarn and you wish the pattern to run uninterrupted, use the other end of the skein, or another color, for working the heel. For the last round before you begin the heel, work needles #1 and #2. The yarn will now be at the beginning of needle #3. If you are using some stitches from the beginning of needle #3 for the heel, work those stitches and transfer them to the end of needle #2. Leave the yarn where it is. Adjust stitches as for the basic heel, and begin working the heel with the new skein. When the next-to-last stitch has been picked up, break the heel yarn, knit with the yarn at needle #3, and finish the basic heel. Return any extra stitches to the instep needle.

Strick-ly Socks

METHOD #2 — THE MEDIUM DECREASE
50% (or more) OF HEEL STITCHES; DELAYED DECREASE IN CUFF

This method works the heel on 50% or more of the stitches, saving the extra gusset stitches to decrease in the first few inches of the cuff. This adds extra room in the instep, ankle, and lower portion of the cuff. If your sock has a center instep pattern that is flanked by stockinette stitch, this is an excellent method to use, as the gusset decreases will not interfere with the pattern.

Place each set of the extra stitches onto each end of the instep needle #3. Work the heel as usual on one-half the total number of stitches. Once the heel turning is complete, decrease 1 stitch on each side of the instep needle every other round when working the sock cuff as follows:

Rnd 1 (needle #3): K1, ssk, knit to 3 stitches before end of instep needle, knit 2tog, k1 — (2 sts dec).
Rnd 2: Work all stitches.

Repeat these 2 rounds for the same number of times you worked the 2 increase rnds for the gusset.

Gusset sts decreased from instep
needle after heel completion

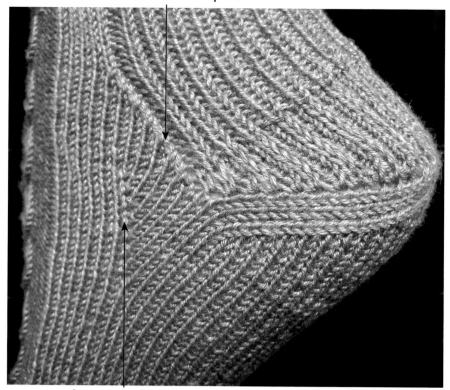

Gusset increases

Butterfly Silk, page 86

METHOD #2 — THE MEDIUM DECREASE
50% (or more) OF HEEL STITCHES; DELAYED DECREASE IN CUFF

If your sock has a continuous pattern around the front and back cuff you can still work that pattern on the original number of stitches, but work the decreases in stockinette stitch. After the decreases have been completed, you can unite the front and back cuff pattern. There will be a small triangular patch of stockinette stitch on each side of the ankle.

You can see how the extra stitches that have been decreased in stockinette stitch barely interfere with the pattern.

Raspberry Trifle stitch pattern, page 66

COMBINATION OF METHODS #1 AND #2 — THE SLOW DECREASE
This method allows for more control over where the stitches are decreased.

The heel can be worked on the usual one-half or more of the total number of stitches plus just a portion of the extra gusset stitches. Once that portion of the extra stitches have been decreased on the underside of the heel, continue the heel as usual. Decrease the extra remaining stitches as for Method #2 by working the decrease row on the instep needle every other row until the extra stitches are gone.

This heel will look like the Method #1 but will be wider and deeper, depending on how many stitches are actually decreased. The decreased triangle of gusset stitches will look like that of Method #2 but smaller.

COMBINATION OF METHODS #2 AND #3 — THE SLOW DECREASE
This method allows for more control over where the stitches are decreased.

The heel can be worked on the usual one-half or more of the total number of stitches. You may then decrease just a portion of the extra gusset stitches as for Method #2. The remaining stitches can be worked with the cuff for extra room.

This heel will look like the Method #2 and the cuff will be wider from the extra stitches that are not decreased.

METHOD #3 — NO DECREASES
50% OF HEEL STITCHES; NO GUSSET STITCHES DECREASED

This method is good to use when the cuff stitch pattern has a tendency to contract width-wise, as in the Smocking Stocking (see page 70). It is also excellent for people with a high instep, larger ankles and/or legs. If your sock recipient requires a wider cuff than what this method yields, you may go up a needle size or two when working the cuff.

Place the extra gusset stitches onto needle #3; work the basic heel on 50% of original stitches.

Smocking Stocking, page 70

Heel Options at a Glance

	No gussets Heel on 50% of sts	No gussets Heel on 60% of sts	Fast Dec #1	Medium Dec #2	Slow Combo Dec	No Dec #3
Average foot	✓	✓	✓			
More instep room		✓	✓	✓	✓	✓
More ankle room				✓	✓	✓
More cuff room					✓	✓
Cuff pattern intact	✓	✓	✓			✓
Stripe/Color sequence uninterrupted if different end used for heel	✓	✓				

Work the cuff in any pattern that is a multiple of the stitch count, until desired length. *(For the directions for making the K1, P1 ribbing with the tubular bind-off see page 32-33.)* Sometimes the stitch count has to be adjusted in order to have an even number of stitches to work the ribbing. This can be done on the first round of ribbing.

If your sock has not ended with ribbing, you will still need a stretchy bind-off, such as the Twice-Knit Bind-Off.

Stretchy Twice-Knit Bind-Off

For a sock cuff that is not finished with ribbing, this bind-off keeps the stitches nice and loose.
Knit 2, *insert left-hand needle through the fronts of these two stitches and knit them together. K1*, repeat between *s until all stitches have been bound off.

Some sock knitters like to make their top ribbing K2, P2. If you follow the handy routine for switching stitches, you can still use the beautiful tubular bind-off.

Switching-Stitches Routine for Bind-Off in Knit 2, Purl 2 Rib

If the sock has ended with knit 2, purl 2 ribbing and a tubular bind-off is desired, one must turn the existing ribbing into knit 1, purl 1 ribbing. Use this clever switching-stitches routine to do it.

Knit 1, *slip the next knit stitch and the next purl stitch purlwise to the right-hand needle. Insert the left-hand needle through the front of the knit stitch, drop the purl stitch off the needle, then pick it up with the tip of the right-hand needle and put it on the tip of the left-hand needle (the knit stitch has crossed over the front of the purl stitch). Purl 1, knit 1 (these are the two stitches that changed places), purl 1, knit 1*, repeat between *s, end with a purl 1.

Now work two rounds in the newly established knit 1, purl 1 ribbing. Bind off in tubular method.

SWITCHING-STITCHES ROUTINE

Step 1
Slip the knit stitch and purl stitch purlwise to RH needle. The knit stitch has to switch places with the purl stitch. The knit stitch will cross over the purl stitch.

Step 2
Insert LH needle through the front of the knit stitch.

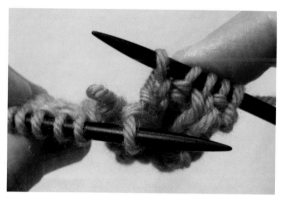

Step 3
Pull the RH needle out; the knit stitch stays on the LH needle, the purl stitch drops behind.

Step 4
With the tip of RH needle pick up the purl stitch and place on the tip of the LH needle; P1, K1.

Step 5
The knit stitch and purl stitch have successfully switched places. When the round has been finished and all stitches are in K1, P1 rib, work 2 rounds in established rib. Bind off.

SWITCHING-STITCHES ROUTINE USING CABLE NEEDLE

If you are afraid of dropping the stitches, you may use a cable needle. Think of it as working a one-over-one cable to the left; the knit stitch crosses to the left over the purl stitch.

Step 1
Slip the knit stitch purlwise to the cable needle and hold in front of work.

Step 2
Purl the purl stitch on the tip of the LH needle; knit the knit stitch from the cable needle.

The knit stitch and purl stitch have successfully switched places. When the round has been finished and all stitches are in K1, P1 rib, work 2 rounds in established rib. Bind off.

Strick-ly Socks

And there you have it—a perfect sock (or pair of socks) constructed using a brand-new method that makes perfect sense!

Now that you have the basics down, I hope you will try your hand at one of the patterns that follow and knit some variations of your own. Some of the greatest pieces of music are variations on a theme, and so are some of the greatest socks. By applying all the techniques of the BOT and TOT formulas, you can vary any part of the sock. It's a whole new world out there, and there are no hard-and-fast rules.

Remember the words of wisdom from the very beginning of the book: Knitting, like life, is a journey of discovery. One can be as daring or as cautious as one feels necessary. The most wonderful thing about knitting is that if you are too daring, and things don't work out, nothing really bad happens.

That's it for socks; stay tuned for *Strick-ly Shawls*, coming soon to a store near you.

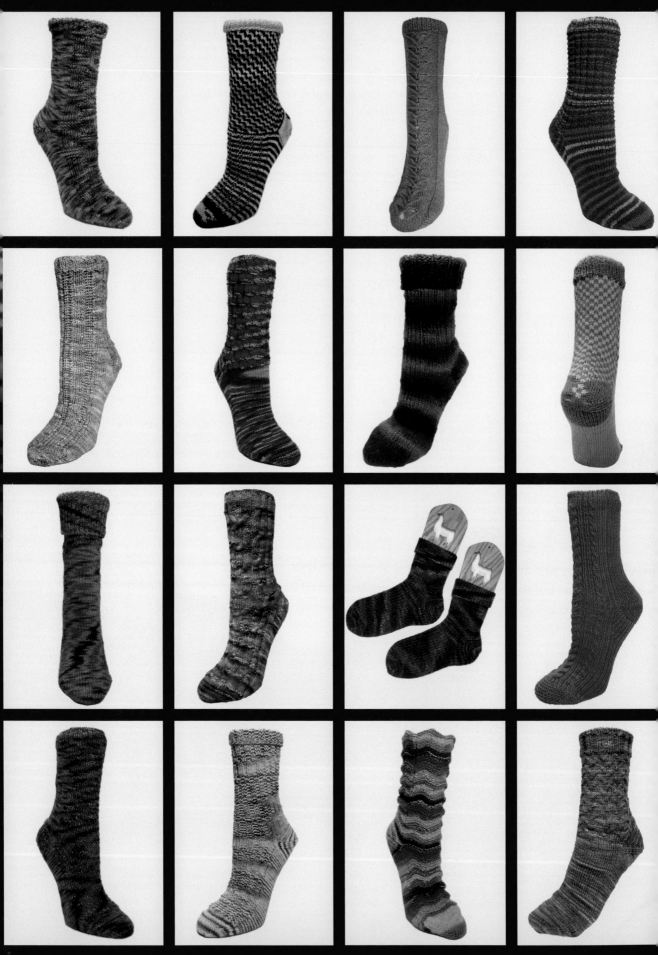

The Patterns

In keeping with the premise of the book, I have purposely kept the patterns simple; they are nonetheless visually compelling. Some of the patterns can be worked by just looking at the fabric that has already been created; others offer easy-to-memorize repeats of cables or stitch designs.

The patterns are written for the toe and heel methods that I used to knit the sock pictured. Each pattern will indicate whether certain parts of the sock need to be an even number or odd number of stitches, a specific multiple, whether there are gussets and how many extra stitches added, and which method I used to use to decrease the extra gusset stitches.

Please feel free to customize the patterns to suit your needs. You may add gussets to any patterns that were knit without them, or vice versa, change the number of gusset stitches to suit your liking, and/or change the method used for decreasing the gusset stitches to fit a particular foot. Or you can omit the gussets and work the heel on more than 50% of the stitches. Because I have a somewhat narrow heel, I decreased the heel underside until it was about 1¼" - 1½", which is about 9, 10, or 11 stitches in sock weight yarn on a size 0 needle. If you wish, you can make your heel wider by working the underside to a greater number of stitches before starting the heel outside.

If you wish to work a BOT sock as TOT, you may do that also. Generally, the TOT socks have a specific toe design, such as Butterfly Silk, which is the reason they are knit in that method. However, many of the other socks can certainly be reverse-engineered.

A few of the patterns use stitch multiples that limit the range of size, such as Raspberry Trifle. In these cases, the number of stitches that the sock needs to be worked on is clearly specified.

A few of the patterns also utilize charts, which are specific for the number of stitches indicated in the directions for "size shown". Even these are easy to modify by deleting or adding stitches along each side of the chart.

Here are the blueprints for easy and totally enjoyable sock knitting. You can follow them exactly or you can make them your own.

Happy Feet Basketweave Socks

This sock is a perfect beginner project. A stretchy basketweave pattern on the instep makes this sock fit well without any gussets. The top ribbing flows organically from the instep pattern.

YARN

2 skeins Plymouth Yarn Co Happy Feet
(90% Superwash merino wool/10% Nylon)
color # 9
[each skein 1.75 oz; 50 gms/192 yds; 177 m]

NEEDLES

Size 0 (2.0 mm) or size needed to obtain gauge

GAUGE 9 sts = 1" in stock st

SIZE SHOWN 64 sts = Adult Medium

PATTERN STITCH

This 21-st patt is worked in the center of the instep sts (odd number); work rem instep sts on each side of center patt in stock st. (The smallest number that works for instep sts is 23.)

Basketweave patt-center 21 sts only

Rnds 1 and 2: K7, (p1, k1)3x, p1, k7.
Rnd 3: P7, (p1, k1)3x, p1, p7.
Rnds 4 and 5: as rnds 1 and 2.
Rnd 6: as rnd 3.
Rnds 7 and 8: as rnds 1 and 2.
Rnd 9: as rnd 3.
Rnd 10 and 11: as rnds 1 and 2.
Rnds 12 and 13: (P1, k1)3x, p1, k7, (p1, k1)3x, p1.
Rnd 14: (P1, k1)3x, p1, k7, (p1, k1)3x, p1.
Rnds 15 and 16: as rnds 12 and 13.
Rnd 17: as rnd 14.
Rnds 18 and 19: as rnds 12 and 13.
Rnd 20: as rnd 14.
Rnds 21 and 22: as rnds 12 and 13.
Rep these 22 rnds for patt. End at cuff top with a completed rnd 11 or 22.

Construction Overview

Construction Method: BOT
Number of sts: at least 46
Instep and Front Cuff sts: odd, center 21 sts in patt; rem in stock st
Back Cuff and Sole sts: even, stock st
Gussets: No
Heel: Basic Heel on 50% (even); underside and outside in GS

CO sts. Work toe in stock st. On first rnd of instep sts dec 1 st for odd number. Work Basketweave patt on center 21 instep sts, working rem instep sts in stock st; work sole sts on even number in stock st.
Work Basic heel in GS on 50% of total sts (even number). When heel is completed, work front cuff in est patt from instep; work back cuff in stock st. Inc 1 st in back cuff on last rnd before top rib. Work K1, P1 rib for desired length, starting rib patt so it lines up with est rib portion of Basketweave from front cuff. BO.

Strick-ly Socks

Short Rib Socks

I used the Louet Hand Dyeing Kit (browns) to color two beautiful skeins for this pair of socks. I worked the instep by switching between 4 rows of K1, P1 rib, and 4 rows of P1, K1 rib. This gives the sock an interesting texture and a nice snug instep. In keeping with the ribbed pattern on the instep, I knit the outside of the heel in rib and worked the underside in smooth stockinette stitch.

Construction Overview
Construction Method: BOT
Number of sts: any
Instep and Front Cuff sts: odd, Broken Rib patt
Back Cuff and Sole sts: odd, stock st
Gussets: No
Heel: Basic Heel on 50% + 1 st (odd); underside stock st; outside P1, K1 rib.

YARN
2 skeins Louet Fingering Weight (100% wool)
[each skein 1.75 oz; 50 gms/185 yds; 170 m]

NEEDLES
Size 0 (2.0 mm) or size needed to obtain gauge

GAUGE 9 sts = 1" in stock st

SIZE SHOWN 64 sts = Adult Medium

PATTERN STITCH
Broken Rib (multiple of 2 sts + 1)
Rows 1, 2, 3, and 4: *K1, p1*, rep between *s to last st, k1.
Rows 5, 6, 7 and 8: *P1, k1*, rep between *s to last st, p1.

CO. Work toe in stock st. On first rnd of instep sts dec 1 st for odd number. Work Broken Rib patt on instep sts; work sole sts in stock st, inc 1 st for odd number. Work underside of heel in stock st. Work outside of heel in P1, K1 rib, working first pu row as: *P1, k1*, rep between *s to end of sts; pu first st in CE as a K st. Next row: work in est rib, pu st in CE as a P st. Cont pu for heel, working new sts into est rib patt. When heel is completed, work front cuff in est patt from instep; work back cuff in stock st. Work cuff to desired length. Work K1, P1 rib in est front cuff patt around entire cuff for desired length. BO.

Who can resist the beautiful colors of a wild Iris?
You can have Spring on your feet all year long.

Construction Overview

Construction Method: BOT
Number of sts: any multiple of 4
Instep sts: even, Rib patt (multiple of 4)
Sole sts: even, stock st
Front and Back Cuff sts: even, Rib patt
(multiple of 4)
Gussets: No
Heel: Basic heel worked on 60% (even);
underside stock st; outside GS

YARN

1 skein Ellen's Half-Pint Farm sock yarn
(75% merino wool/25% nylon), color Wild Iris
(each skein 3.5 oz; 100 gms/462 yds; 426 m)

NEEDLES

Size 0 (2.0) or size needed to obtain gauge

GAUGE 8 sts = 1" in stock st

SIZE SHOWN 64 sts = Adult Medium

PATTERN STITCH

Rib Pattern (multiple of 4)
Rnds 1, 2, 3, 4, 5, 6, 7, 8, 9, and 10:
P1, *k2, p2*, rep between *s until 3 sts rem, k2, p1.
Rnds 11, 12, 13, and 14: K1 *p2, k2*, rep
between *s until 3 sts rem, p2, k1.

CO sts. Work toe topside and underside in
stock st. Work instep sts in Rib patt; work
sole in stock st. Work basic heel on 60% of
sts; work underside of heel in stock st; work
outside heel in GS. When heel is completed
return extra sts used for heel to each end of
instep needle and cont in est patt. Work
back cuff in Rib patt until desired length,
ending cuff with completed rnd 10. Work
Switching-Stitches Routine. BO.

Jumpin' Bungee Socks

These stretchy little treasures work up in a jiffy. The waffle stitch on the cuff looks far more intricate than it really is, and the stretch of the yarn, combined with the stitch pattern, is fantastic! Because the yarn is a bit thicker than traditional sock yarn, I used size 2 (2.75 mm) needles. This sock is perfect for getting your feet wet with the new method.

Construction Overview
Construction Method: BOT
Number of sts: any
Instep and Sole sts: even, stock st
Front and Back cuff sts: Waffle patt (multiple of 3)
Gussets: No
Heel: Basic Heel on 50% (even); underside and outside stock st

YARN
1 skein Plymouth Yarn Co Bungee
(95% Merino Wool/5% Elite Spandex), color #617
[each skein 3.5 oz; 100 gms/403 yds; 372 m]

NEEDLES
Size 2 (2.75 mm) or size needed to obtain gauge

GAUGE 7 sts = 1" in stock st

SIZE SHOWN 56 sts = Adult Medium

PATTERN STITCH
Waffle patt (multiple of 3)
Rnds 1, 2 and 3: *K2, p1*, rep between *s.
Rnd 4: Purl.

CO. Work toe, foot, and heel (50% of sts) in stock st on even number of sts. When heel is completed, inc or dec as necessary in first rnd of Waffle patt to multiple of 3. Work cuff in Waffle patt until desired length, ending with completed rnd 4, dec or inc 1 st in this last rnd to multiple of 2. Work in K1, P1 rib for desired length. BO.

Strick-ly Socks

Mr Congeniality

I set out to knit a reversible sock for the sheer fun of it. In order to keep the rib pattern in perfect order while working the gussets, I increased 2 sts on each side of the sole every 4 rounds. With the heels and toes in garter stitch, this sock is totally congenial on both sides!

Construction Overview
Construction Method: BOT
Number of sts: any
Instep and Front Cuff sts: even; K1, P1 rib patt
Back Cuff and Sole sts: even; K1, P1 rib patt
Gussets: Yes, 16 sts (special increase instructions included in directions)
Heel: Method #1 worked on 50% of sts + gusset sts (even) in GS

YARN
1 skein Blue Moon Fiber Arts Socks That Rock Medium Weight (100% Superwash Wool)
color Puck's Mischief
[each skein, 5.5 oz; 156 gm/ 360 yds; 347 m]

NEEDLES
Size 0 (2.0 mm) or size needed to obtain gauge

GAUGE
10 sts = 1" in K1, P1 rib patt **unstretched**

SIZE SHOWN 64 sts = Adult Men's Medium

PATTERN STITCH
K1, P1 rib (multiple of 2)
All rnds: *K1, p1*, rep between *s.
GS (worked flat for toes and heels)
K all rows.

CO. Work toe in GS. Work instep and sole in K1, P1 rib patt until foot is 16 rnds before beg of heel. Work the foll 4 rnds 4 times on sole sts for gusset incs:
Rnd 1: K1, M1P, K next st which is a P st, M1P, work patt to last 2 sole sts, M1L, P next st which is a K st, M1L, P last st.
Rnds 2, 3, and 4: Work in est patt.
Work heel Method #1 in GS.
Work cuff in est patt to desired length. BO.

Tip: Because the toe is worked in GS, it is easy to confuse RS and WS. Make sure to mark RS of your work.

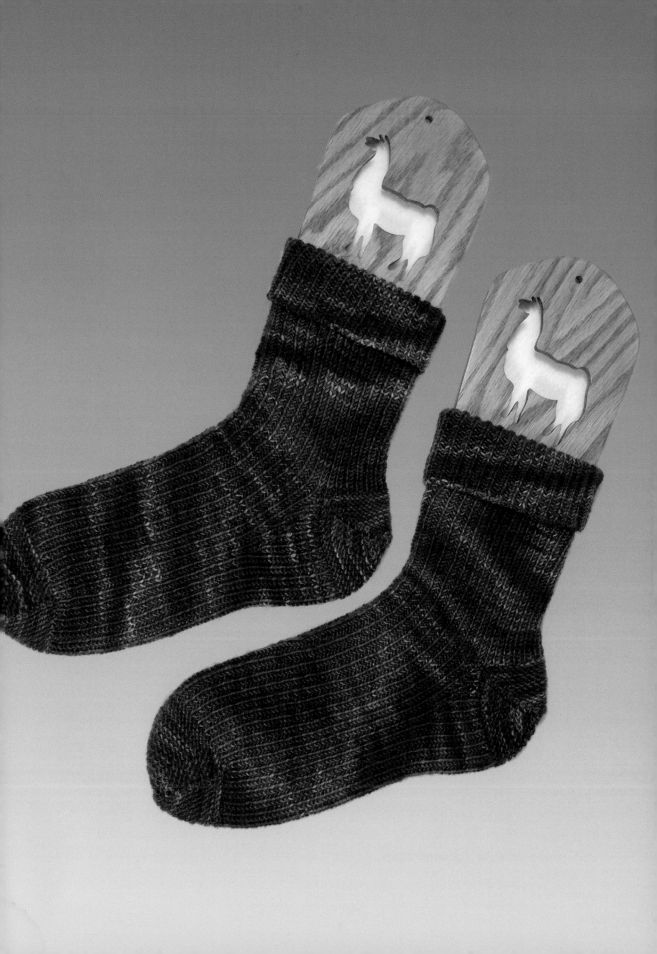

Ms Congeniality

Not to be outdone by Mr Congeniality, Ms Congeniality is also a totally reversible sock, but with pretty feminine cables gracing the instep and front cuff. You may work the cuff longer and turn it down if you wish, as the cables look perfect from either side. This sock requires a minimum of 28 instep stitches for the cable pattern.

Construction Overview

Construction Method: BOT
Number of sts: 56 (64, 72, 80)
Instep and Front Cuff sts: even, Cable patt
Back Cuff and Sole sts: even; K1, P1 rib patt
Gussets: Yes, 16 sts (special increase instructions included in directions)
Heel: Method #1 worked on 50% of sts + gusset sts (even) in GS

YARN

2 skeins Louet Fingering Weight (100% wool) color Crabapple
[each skein 1.75 oz; 50 gms/185 yds; 170 m]

NEEDLES

Size 0 (2.0 mm) or size needed to obtain gauge

GAUGE

11 sts = 1" in K1, P1 rib patt *unstretched*

SIZE SHOWN 64 sts = Adult Medium

PATTERN STITCH

K1, P1 rib (multiple of 2)
All rnds: *K1, p1*, rep between *s.

GS (worked flat for toes and heels)
K all rows.

Cable pattern

Rnds 1, 2, 3, 4, and 5: *K1, p1*, rep between *s.
Rnd 6: *K1, p1* rep between *s 1 (2, 3, 4) times, k1, p1, slip next 2 sts to cn and hold in back of work, k1, p1 from LH needle, k1, p1 from cn (cable turned to right), k1, p1, k1, p1, slip next 4 sts to cn and hold front of work, k1, p1, k1, p1 from LH needle, k1, p1, k1, p1 from cn (center cable turned to left), k1, p1, k1, p1, slip next 2 sts to cn and hold in front of work, k1, p1 from LH needle, k1, p1 from cn (cable turned to left), finish instep sts with *k1, p1* rep between *s 1 (2, 3, 4) times.
Rnds 7, 8, 9, 10 and 11: *K1, p1*, rep between *s.
Rnd 12: As rnd 6.
Rep these 12 rnds for Cable patt.

CO 28 (32, 36, 40) sts. Work sock exactly as for Mr Congenialty, but working Cable patt on 28 (32, 36, 40) instep sts and front cuff. Work sole and back cuff in K1, P1 rib patt. Work until desired length, ending with completed rnd 6 or 12 of Cable patt. Work 8 rnds of est K1, P1 rib patt. BO.

Variations

The cable patt can also be worked on the back cuff.

For the second sock, you may reverse the center cable so it turns to the right (slip next 4 sts to cn and hold in back of work, k1, p1, k1, p1 from LH needle, k1, p1, k1, p1 from cn).

Strick-ly Socks

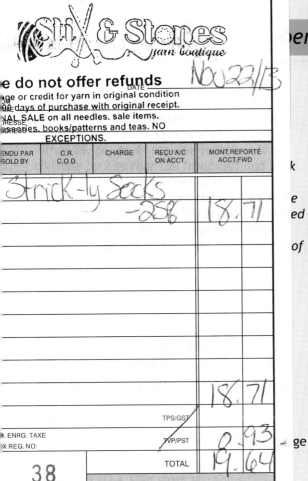

erry Trifle

Construction Overview
Construction Method: TOT
Number of sts: 44, 66, 88
Instep, Front Cuff and Back Cuff sts: multiple of 11, Ripple Wave patt
Sole sts: multiple of 11, stock st
Gussets: No
Heel: Basic Heel on 60% of total sts; underside stock st; outside GS

CO 10 sts. Work toe topside in stock st until 22 (34, 44) sts. Work toe underside in stock st until 22 (34, 44) sts. Dec 0 (1, 0) st on instep sts on first rnd; work instep in Ripple Wave patt; dec 0 (1, 0) st on sole sts; work sole sts in stock st. On last rnd before heel work sole sts (needles #1 and #2), and 2 (3, 2) sts of instep needle. Leave this yarn here, as it will be used when the heel is completed. The heel will be worked on 26 (39, 48) sts with a new ball of yarn. Transfer 2 (3, 2) sts from each end of the instep needle to the end of needle #2 and to the beginning of needle #1.

Work basic heel until there is 1 less st than original number. Break the heel yarn. Work across the instep sts with original yarn. At beg of next rnd pu the last st that is needed. Transfer the 2 (3, 2) sts from each end of sole sts back to each end of instep needle. Work Ripple Wave patt on back cuff and front cuff until desired length, ending with a completed rnd 12. Work the foll 5 rnds:

Rnds 1, 3 and 5: Purl.
Rnds 2 and 4: *K2tog, k2, knit into the front and back of the next 2 sts, k3, ssk*, rep between *s.

BO in Stretchy Twice-Knit BO. (See page 48)

SIZE SHOWN 66 sts = Adult Medium

PATTERN STITCH
Ripple Wave (multiple of 11)
Rnds 1, 3, and 5: Purl.
Rnds 2 and 4: Knit.
Rnds 6, 8 and 10: *K2tog, k2, knit into front and back of next 2 sts, k3, ssk*, rep between *s.
Rnds 7, 9, and 11: Knit.
Rnd 12: *K2tog, k2, knit into front and back of next 2 sts, k3, ssk*, rep between *s.

Tip. If working gussets, work heel Method #2. Decreasing the extra stitches will briefly interrupt the pattern, but is barely noticeable. (See page 46)

Purple Lightning Socks

As I was knitting these socks, a lightning bolt started to appear in the purple dyed portions of the yarn. It's always fun to see what happens with hand-dyed yarn. I worked the outside of the heel in Slip-Stitch Heel pattern for durability. You may fold down the long ribbed cuff if you wish.

Construction Overview
Construction Method: BOT
Number of sts: any
Instep and Front Cuff sts: even, stock st
Back Cuff and Sole sts: even, stock st
Gussets: Yes, 14 sts
Heel: Method #2 worked on 50% of sts + 1 st (odd); underside stock st, outside Slip-Stitch Heel patt

YARN
2 skeins Louet Fingering Weight
(100% wool) hand-dyed by author
[each skein 1.75 oz; 50 gms/185 yds; 170 m]

NEEDLES
Size 0 (2.0 mm) or size needed to obtain gauge

GAUGE 9 sts = 1" in stock st

SIZE SHOWN 64 sts = Adult Medium

PATTERN STITCH
K1, P1 rib (multiple of 2)
All rnds: *K1, p1*, rep between *s.

CO. Work toe in stock st. Work instep and sole in stock st, inc 1 st in sole sts for odd number. Work until foot is 14 rounds before beg of heel. Work gusset inc every other rnd 7 times.

Work heel Method #2 underside in stock st; outside in Slip-Stitch Heel patt on odd number.

When heel is completed work front and back cuff in stock st, dec extra sts every other rnd on instep needle as for heel Method #2.

Cont cuff until stock st measures 2" or desired length; dec 1 st on last row. Work K1, P1 rib for 5 ½" or desired length. BO.

Smocking Stocking

This sock pattern had its debut in 2003 when I started my pattern company, *Strickwear*. However, in its original form it was worked as a top-down sock with a conventional heel flap. Because the Smocking pattern has a tendency to pull in tightly, the sock cuff needed many more extra stitches, and the gusset stitches happened to be the magic number. Instead of decreasing the extra stitches as in most socks, I incorporated them into the Smocking pattern. Diane Lutz dyed a skein of her gorgeous yarn in screaming acid green, shocking pink, glaring red, and neon blue. It was love at first sight!

YARN
1 skein Creatively Dyed Yarn Steele (100% Superwash merino), color Albion [each skein 6.75 oz; 189 gms/500 yds; 461 m]

NEEDLES
Size 0 (2.0 mm) or size needed to obtain gauge

GAUGE 8 sts = 1" in stock st

SIZE SHOWN
64 sts foot/80 sts cuff = Adult Medium
72 sts foot/88 sts cuff = Adult L

Construction Overview
Construction Method: BOT
Number of sts: 64 (72)
Instep sts: even, stock st
Sole sts: even, stock st
Cuff sts: 80 (88) sts in Smocking patt
Gussets: Yes, 16 sts
Heel: Method #3 worked on 50% of sts (even); stock st

PATTERN STITCH
Smocking Pattern (multiple of 8)
Rnds 1-6: *K2, p2*, rep between *s to end.
Rnd 7: *Insert RH needle from front between 6th and 7th sts on LH needle and draw through a loop, slip this loop onto LH needle and k it tog with the first st, k1, p2, k2, p2*, rep between *s to end.
Rnds 8-12: *K2, p2*, rep between *s to end.
Rnd 13: *K2, p2* rep between *s to last 4 sts. Place marker here for beg/end of rnd. Place last 4 sts on next needle.
Rnd 14: Work as for rnd 4, adjusting sts on needles as necessary.
Rep rnds 8-14 for patt.

CO on 32 (36) sts. Work toe in stock st. Work instep and sole in stock st until foot is 16 rnds before beg of heel. Work gusset inc every other rnd 8 times. Put the 16 extra sts (8 are on each side of sole sts) onto each end of instep needle. Work heel in Method #3 in stock st on 32 (36) sts. After heel has been completed work 1 rnd in stock st, stopping 8 sts before end of rnd. Place a marker here for beg/end of rnd. If desired, distribute sts more evenly onto needles. Do not dec any gusset sts. Work cuff in Smocking Pattern on 80 (88) sts until 1" from desired length. Work rnds 1-6. Work Switching-Stitches Routine. BO.

Howard Johnson

Remember the bright orange roof and the turquoise booths? This sock has a clever alternating cable pattern that gives the cuff an interesting texture. Because the cables tend to tighten up the stitch pattern, I kept the gusset stitches for use in the cuff.

YARN
1 skein Ellen's Half-Pint Farm sock yarn (100% merino wool), color Orange/Turquoise [each skein 4 oz; 112 gms/500 yds; 462 m]

NEEDLES
Size 0 (2.0 mm) or size needed to obtain gauge

GAUGE 9 sts = 1" in stock st

SIZE SHOWN
64 sts = Adult Medium

PATTERN STITCH
Cable Pattern (multiple of 8)
Rnds 1, 2, and 3: Knit.
Rnd 4: *Slip 2 sts to cn and hold in back of work, knit 2 sts from LH needle, knit the 2 sts from cn, knit 4*, rep between *s.
Rnds 5, 6, and 7: Knit.
Rnd 8: *K4, slip 2 sts to cn and hold in front of work, knit 2 sts from LH needle, knit the 2 sts from cn*, rep between *s.
Rep these 8 rnds for patt.

CO sts. Work toe in stock st; work foot in stock st until 16 rnds before beg of heel. Work gusset inc every other rnd 8 times. Work heel Method #3 in stock st. Rep the 8 rnds of Cable patt for cuff until desired length, ending with a completed rnd 2 or 6. Knit 1 rnd, dec 16 sts evenly spaced. Work in K2, P2 rib until desired length. Work Switching-Stitches Routine. BO.

A One-Night Stand with Mochi Plus

The beautiful color transitions and softness of this yarn seduced me so much that I was able to complete a sock in one night. Thick and cozy for wearing inside, these socks incorporate heel Method #2, which decreases the extra gusset stitches after heel completion. Because this yarn gradually merges from one color to the next, I used a new ball of yarn for the heel to avoid an obvious color shift on the instep. The 3 X 1 Rib pattern is totally reversible, allowing you to turn down the cuff.

Construction Overview

Construction Method: TOT
Number of sts: any
Instep sts: even, stock st
Sole sts: even, stock st
Cuff sts: even, stock st and 3 X 1 Rib patt
Gussets: Yes, 6 sts
Heel: Method #2 worked on 50% + 1 (odd); underside in stock st, outside in Slip-Stitch Heel patt

YARN

3 skeins Crystal Palace Yarns Mochi Plus (80% merino wool/20% nylon), color #553 [each skein 1.75 oz; 50 gms/95 yds; 87 m]

NEEDLES

Size 4 (3.5) needles or size needed to obtain gauge

GAUGE 6 sts = 1" in stock st

SIZE SHOWN 48 sts = Adult Women's Medium

PATTERN STITCH
3 X 1 rib (multiple of 4)
All rnds: *K3, p1*, rep between *s.

CO 6 sts. Work toe in stock st until desired size. Work foot in stock st, inc 1 st on sole sts. Work until foot is 6 rnds before beg of heel.

Work gusset inc every other rnd 3 times. Leave original yarn here.

Using another ball of yarn for heel, work first heel st in new yarn. Slip st back to LH needle and work heel Method #2 underside in stock st. Work outside heel in Slip-Stitch Heel patt.

For last RS row of heel, break yarn, cont with original yarn. Work in stock st while dec extra sts as for heel Method #2, then switch to 3 X 1 rib patt, inc as necessary for a multiple of 4. Work to desired length; work 2 rnds of K1, P1 rib, BO. To wear, fold down top about 2".

My friend, Dianne Lutz, dyes beautiful skeins for her company Creatively Dyed Yarns. These socks were inspired by a particularly fiery skein she gave me. Because of the stretchy nature of the ribbing, I had to do only 6 gusset increases instead of the usual 7 or 8. I also kept a border of 3 garter sts on each side of the heel, which makes an interesting variation.

Construction Overview
Construction Method: BOT
Number of sts: 64 (72, 80) sts
Instep and Front Cuff sts: even, Cable patt
Sole sts: even
Back Cuff sts: K2, P2 rib patt (multiple of 4)
Gussets: Yes, 12 sts
Heel: Method #1 worked on 50% of sts + gusset sts (even) in stock st with 3 st GS border

YARN 1 skein Creatively Dyed Yarn Calypso (100% Superwash merino), color name: Blocks [each skein 6.75 oz; 189 gms/500 yds; 461 m]

NEEDLES
Size 0 (2.0 mm) or size needed to obtain gauge

GAUGE 8.5 sts = 1" in stock st

SIZE SHOWN 64 sts =Adult Medium

OTHER SIZES 72 sts = Adult L
                 80 sts = Adult XL

PATTERN STITCH
K2, P2 rib (multiple of 4)
All rnds: *K2, p2*, rep between *s.
Cable pattern
Chart of 17 rnds; 32 (36, 40) sts

CO 32 (36, 40) sts. Work toe in stock st.

Est patt: K sole sts, work instep sts as rnd 2 of chart for your size 5 times. Beg on rnd 1, work instep sts foll chart for your size; work sole sts in stock st. Work until foot is 12 rnds before beg of heel. Work gusset inc every other rnd 6 times. (Mark last completed rnd, as you will need to cont in est patt after heel completion.) Work heel Method #1 in stock st, working first 3 sts and last 3 sts in GS, and remembering to work CE for GS at beg of every row. When heel is completed, cont working around cuff, working front cuff in est instep Cable patt. Rep rnd 2 of chart for back cuff.

Work until cuff is desired length ending with completed rnd 16 Cable patt. Work in est K2, P2 rib until desired length.

Adjust sts between needle #3 and needle #1 as necessary to make rnd beg with K2. Work Switching-Stitches Routine. BO.

Variation: I twisted the 3-over-3 cable to the right on one sock, and to the left on its mate. You can alternate left and right on the same sock if you like. You can also alternate the smaller side cables.

Flaming Cables Instep and Front Cuff (Rep 16 rnds for patt)

I Knit **—** Purl

Slip 2 to CN, hold in back, k2, k2 from CN

Slip 2 to CN, hold in front, p1, k2 from CN

Slip 2 to CN, hold in front, k2, k2 from CN

Slip 1 to CN, hold in back, k2, p1 from CN

Slip 3 to CN, hold in front, k3, k3 from CN

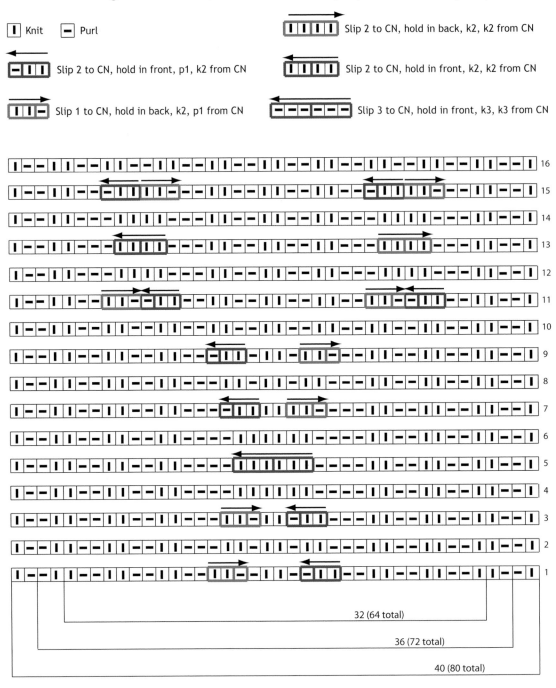

32 (64 total)

36 (72 total)

40 (80 total)

Baby Mochi

You can make these wee baby socks from the leftovers of Adult Mochi.

Construction Overview
Construction Method: BOT
Number of sts: any
Instep sts: even, stock st
Sole sts: even, stock st
Cuff: even, stock st and K1, P1 rib patt
Gussets: No
Heel: Basic heel worked on 50% (even); underside and outside in stock st

YARN
25 gms Crystal Palace Yarns Mochi Plus
(80% merino wool/20% nylon), color #553
[each skein 1.75 oz; 50 gms/95 yds; 87 m]

NEEDLES
Size 4 (3.5) needles or size needed to obtain gauge

GAUGE 6 sts = 1" in stock st

SIZE SHOWN 28 sts = Baby

PATTERN STITCH
K1, P1 rib (multiple of 2)
All rnds: *K1, p1*, rep between *s.

CO sts. Work toe in stock st to 6 sts (last dec row will be worked as CE, k1, ssk, k2tog, k2). Work foot in stock st. Work basic heel in stock st on 50% of sts. Cont cuff in stock st for 2", then work in K1, P1 rib for 2 ½". BO.

Spring Chicken

This beautiful yarn inspired me to knit something spring-like, and a pretty lace pattern immediately came to mind. In keeping with the little lace pattern on the toe, I worked the toe increases as yarn-overs but did not close them up on the wrong-side rows.

Construction Overview
Construction Method: TOT
Number of sts: 55
Instep and Front Cuff sts: odd, patt from chart
Sole sts: even, stock st
Back Cuff sts: even; P1, *k2, p2* rep between *s to last 3 sts, k2, p1
Gussets: yes, 16 sts
Heel: Method #2 worked on 62% (34 sts); underside and outside stock st

YARN
1 skein Miss Babs Hand-dyed Yarns and Fibers (100% superwash merino wool), color Bluegrass [each skein 4 oz; 112 gms/400 yds; 369 m]

NEEDLES
Size 0 (2.0 mm) or size needed to obtain gauge

GAUGE 9 sts = 1" in stock st

SIZE SHOWN 55 sts = Adult Medium

PATTERN STITCH (cuff and foot)
Vertical Lace (multiple of 5)
Rnd 1: K2tog, yo, k1, ssk.
Rnd 2: Knit

Note: This vertical lace pattern has a tendency to spread out because of the yarn-overs. I discovered that 55 sts fit perfectly, whereas I usually need 64 sts with a non-lace design. If you wish to make your sock bigger, add as many extra stitches on each side of the lace patt as you wish; if you wish your sock smaller, work less sts on each side of the lace patt. You may have to adjust the back cuff rib patt.

CO 10 sts. Work toe chart to 27 sts. Work underside of toe in stock st. Work instep in patt from chart until foot is 16 rnds before beg of heel. Work gusset inc every other rnd 8 times. Work heel Method #2 in stock st on 34 sts. Cont instep patt as est for front cuff, work back cuff in rib patt until desired length, ending with a completed rnd 2 of lace patt. For next rnd work back cuff in est rib patt, work front cuff in same rib patt, inc 1 st at end of rnd by Kfb. Cont in K2, P2 Rib patt until desired length. Work Switching-Stitches routine. BO.

Spring Chicken Charts

Knit

Instep and Front Cuff

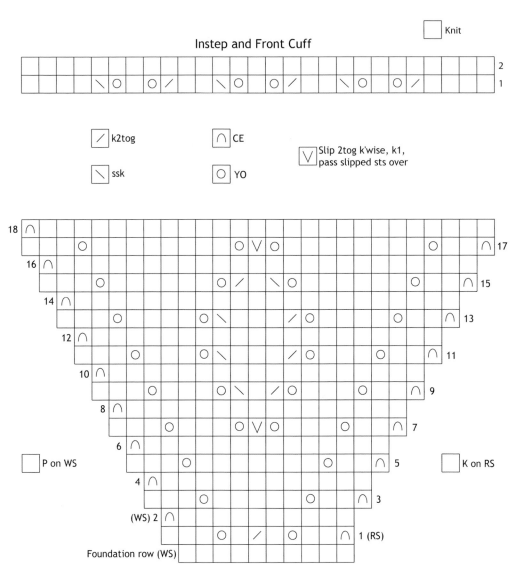

| / | k2tog | | ∩ | CE |
| \ | ssk | | O | YO |

V Slip 2tog k'wise, k1, pass slipped sts over

P on WS

K on RS

Toe

Alien Abduction

The shocking green yarn reminded me of little aliens. When paired with black yarn, the high contrast made the easy slip-stitch pattern pop. For the second sock I decided to knit an alien sheep on the toe and outside heel.

YARN

1 skein Zitron Trekking XXL (75% wool, 25% Nylon)
Green 401 [each skein 3.5 oz; 100 gms/459 yds; 424m]

1 skein Cascade Yarns Heritage
(75% Merino Superwash/25% Nylon)
Black 5601 [each skein 3.5 oz; 100 gms/437 yds; 403m]

NEEDLES

Size 0 (2.0) or size needed to obtain gauge

GAUGE 9 sts = 1" in stock st

SIZE SHOWN

64 sts foot/80 sts cuff = Adult Medium

PATTERN STITCH

Rib pattern (multiple of 4)

Rnds 1 and 2: (Black) P1, *k2, p2* rep between *s to last 3 sts, k2, p1.
Rnds 3 and 4: (Green) Work as rnds 1 and 2.

Rick Rack pattern (multiple of 4)

All stitches are slipped purlwise wyib.

Rnds 1 and 2: With Green, k1, *slip 1, k3*, rep between *s to last 3 sts, slip 1, k2.
Rnds 3 and 4: With Black *slip 1, k3*, rep between *s.
Rnds 5 and 6: With Green, *k3, slip 1*, rep between *s.
Rnds 7 and 8: With Black, k2, *slip 1, k3*, rep between *s to last 2 sts, slip 1, k1.

Construction Overview

Construction Method: TOT
Number of sts: any multiple of 4
Instep sts: even, Rib patt (multiple of 4); alternate 2 rnds Green, 2 rnds Black
Sole sts: even, stock st; alternate 2 rnds Green, 2 rnds Black
Front and Back Cuff sts: Rick Rack patt (multiple of 4)
Gussets: Yes, 16 sts
Heel: Method #3 on 50% of sts (even); underside and outside stock st

---

CO 10 sts with Black; work toe in stock st, working patt from chart if desired. Work instep in Rib patt beg with Green; work sole in stock st alternating 2 rnds of each color. Work until foot is 16 rnds before beg of heel. Work gusset inc every other rnd 8 times.
Heel: If last rnd before heel is Green, work heel in Black. If last rnd before heel is Black, work heel in Green. Work patt from chart for heel outside if desired.
Keep color not in use attached. It is at the end of needle #3.
Work heel Method #3 in stock st.
If heel is worked in Black, work one more rnd after heel has been completed, working instep sts in est patt. Begin Rick Rack patt for cuff.
If heel is worked in Green, work outside heel until there are 2 sts less than one-half the total number. Change to Black and complete heel. Begin Rick Rack patt for cuff.
Work cuff to desired length. Knit 1 rnd in Green, dec 16 sts evenly spaced. Work K1, P1 rib in Green for desired length. BO.

Strick-ly Socks

Alien Abduction Charts

Toe

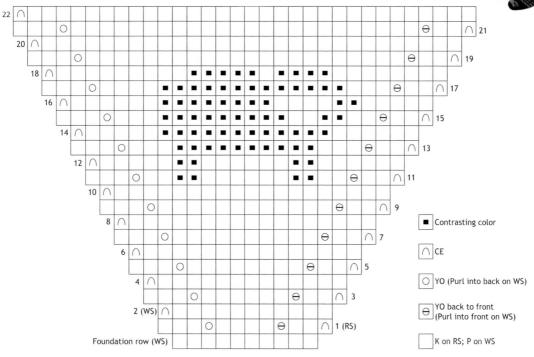

Foundation row (WS)

Symbol	Meaning
■	Contrasting color
∩	CE
○	YO (Purl into back on WS)
⊖	YO back to front (Purl into front on WS)
□	K on RS; P on WS

Last stitch to pick-up in CE before uniting to rnd

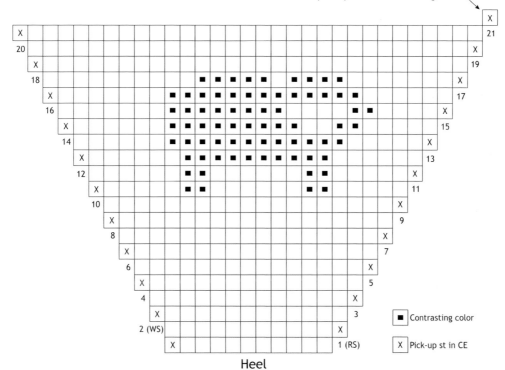

Symbol	Meaning
■	Contrasting color
X	Pick-up st in CE

Heel

Butterfly Silk

This beautiful pattern is a 10-row-repeat that is easily memorized. There are two sets of directions for the pattern stitch. Follow the back-and-forth directions when working the toe; follow the in-the-round directions when working the instep and cuff. The back cuff is worked in K1, P1 ribbing, which flows beautifully from the Slip-Stitch Heel pattern. Worked in Panda Silk, this sock is worthy of royalty.

YARN
2 skeins Crystal Palace Yarns Panda Silk (52% bamboo/43% superwash merino wool/5% combed silk), color #3006 [each skein 1.75 oz; 50 gms/204 yds; 188 m]

NEEDLES
Size 0 (2.0 mm) or size needed to obtain gauge

Construction Overview
Construction Method: TOT
Number of Stitches: at least 32
Instep and Front Cuff sts: even, center 16 sts in Butterfly patt flanked on each side by p3; rem sts in stock st
Sole sts: odd, stock st
Back Cuff: even, K1, P1 rib
Gussets: Yes, 14 sts
Heel: Method #2 on 50% of sts +1 (odd); underside stock st; outside Slip-Stitch Heel patt

GAUGE 9 sts = 1" in stock st

SIZE SHOWN 64 sts = Adult Medium

PATTERN STITCH
Butterfly pattern (panel of 16 sts)
(See shaded boxes.)

Butterfly pattern for toe worked back-and-forth

WS left leaning decrease (WS-lld) is worked as follows:
P1, wyif slip next st knitwise, slip both sts purlwise back to LH needle, pass the slip st over the purl st, put the rem st on RH needle.

Drop the yo's from previous rows before making the yo's for the row you are on.

Row 1 (RS): P1, k5, k2tog, (yo)2x, ssk, k5, p1.
Row 2: K1, p4, WS-lld, (yo) 2x, p2tog, p4, k1.
Row 3: P1, k3, k2tog, (yo) 2x, ssk, k3, p1.
Row 4: K1, p2, WS-lld, (yo) 2x, p2tog, p2, k1.
Row 5: P1, k1, k2tog, (yo) 2x, ssk, k1, p1.
Row 6: K1, WS-lld, (yo) 2x, p2tog, k1.
Row 7: P1, k1, e-loop CO 5 sts onto RH needle, **lift loop**, e-loop CO 6 sts onto RH needle, k1, p1.
Row 8: K1, p14, k1—16 sts.
Row 9: P1, k14, p1.
Row 10: as row 8

to lift loops, with RH needle go under the strands from bottom to top, wrap yarn around needle and pull it under the loops, lifting them all up and making a st on the needle.

See photos for e-loop CO and lift loop.

Butterfly pattern for instep and front cuff in-the-round

Drop the yo's from previous rows before making the yo's for the row you are on.
Panel of 16 sts.
Row 1 (RS): *P1, k5, k2tog, (yo)2x, ssk, k5, p1*, rep between *s.
Row 2: *P1, k4, k2tog, (yo) 2x, ssk, k4, p1*, rep between *s.
Row 3: *P1, k3, k2tog, (yo) 2x, ssk, k3, p1*, rep between *s.
Row 4: *P1, k2, k2tog, (yo) 2x, ssk, k2, p1*, rep between *s.
Row 5: *P1, k1, k2tog, (yo) 2x, ssk, k1, p1*, rep between *s.
Row 6: *P1, k2tog, (yo) 2x, ssk, k1*, rep between *s.
Row 7: *P1, k1, e-loop CO 5 sts onto RH needle, **lift loop**, e-loop CO 6 sts onto RH needle, k1, p1*, rep between *s
Rows 8, 9, and 10: *P1, k14, p1*, rep between *s—16 sts.
Repeat these 10 rows for pattern.

to lift loops, with RH needle go under the strands from bottom to top, wrap yarn around needle and pull it under the loops, lifting them all up and making a st on the needle.

See photos for e-loop CO and lift loop

CO 10 sts. Work toe topside in stock st until 24 sts. Beg Butterfly patt back and forth on center 16 sts, starting on a RS row. As sts are inc for toe, add 3 extra purls on each side of center panel as sts become available. Once there are 3 purls on each side of center panel *(remember there is 1 purl on each end of Butterfly patt, so once there are 3 purls on each side, you will actually see 4 purls in a row)*, work rem sts in stock st until toe has desired number of sts. Work toe underside in stock st. When toe is completed cont working Butterfly patt up instep sts, remembering to work directions for in-the-rnd; work sole sts in stock st, inc 1 st in sole sts for odd number. Work until foot is 14 rnds before beg of heel. Work gusset inc every other rnd 7 times. Work heel Method #2, working underside in stock st; work outside heel in Slip-Stitch Heel patt. After last st of heel has been picked up, knit first rnd of back cuff, then work in P1, K1 rib, beg with P1 so it lines up nicely with Slip-St Heel patt. Work cuff until desired length. Work ending K1, P1 rib on entire cuff in est patt from back cuff, inc 1 st in front cuff to make rib come out even. BO.

Tip: You could work more than 3 purls on each side of the center panel, or less purls.

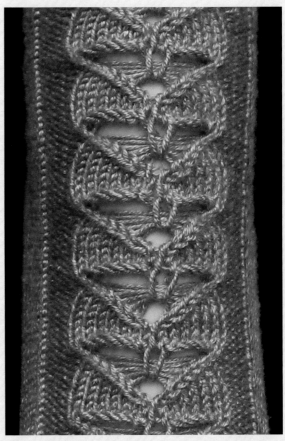

Step 1
Row 7: There are 6 bars of yarn that were YO's from previous rows; ready to e-loop cast on 5 stitches onto RH needle.

Step 2
To e-loop cast on, wrap yarn from back to front around index finger.

Step 3
To make the stitch, insert RH needle through loop and tighten. Cast on 5 stitches this way.

Step 4
Five e-loop cast on stitches finished; ready to lift loops.

Step 5
To lift loops, insert RH needle under all loops from bottom to top.

Step 6
Wrap yarn around needle and pull up a stitch under the loops, lifting them all up and making a stitch on the needle.

Step 7
A finished lifted loop.

Step 8
E-loop cast on 6 stitches to finish the butterfly.

I love the trick of reversing colors to make a positive/negative pair. Because two-color knitting tends to draw in, this sock keeps the gusset stitches for use in the cuff. After knitting one pair as specified, you will have enough yarn left over to knit another pair of socks in any pattern that uses equal amounts of two colors.

Construction Overview

Construction Method: BOT
Number of sts: 64
Instep sts: even
Front Cuff and Back Cuff sts: multiple of 4
Sole sts: even, stock st
Gussets: Yes, 16 sts
Heel: Method #3 on 60% of sts; underside and outside stock st

YARN

2 skeins Cascade Yarns Heritage Sock Yarn
1 each Turquoise #5630 and Lavender #5614
(75% Superwash wool/25% nylon)
[each skein 3.5 oz; 100 gms/437 yds; 400 m]

NEEDLES

Size 0 (2.0 mm) or size needed to obtain gauge

GAUGE 9 sts = 1" in stock st

SIZE SHOWN 64 sts = Adult Medium

PATTERN STITCH

Stockinette Stitch
Worked back and forth: K on RS; P on WS
Worked in the rnd: K every rnd

Sock #1

With Turquoise CO 32 sts. Work toe chart until 10 sts rem. Work toe underside. When all sts are picked up attach Lavender; work foot until 16 rows before beg of heel. Work gusset inc every other rnd 8 times. Work heel Method #3 underside on 60% of sts (36 sts) in Turquoise until 10 sts rem. Follow heel chart for outside of heel.

Work cuff on 80 sts in the foll patt:
Rnds 1 and 2: *K2 Turquoise, k2 Lavender*, rep between *s.
Rnds 3 and 4: *K2 Lavender, k2 Turquoise*, rep between *s.

Work until cuff is desired length, ending with a completed rnd 2 or 4.

Knit 1 rnd with Turquoise, dec 16 sts evenly spaced. Work top rib as K1, P1 in Turquoise until desired length. Knit 1 rnd with Lavender. Work 2 rnds of est rib in Lavender. BO with Lavender.

Sock #2

Work as for sock #1 reversing all colors.

Positively Negative Charts

Topside Toe

Legend:
- □ K on RS; P on WS
- ■ Contrasting color
- ∩ CE
- \ SSK
- / K2tog

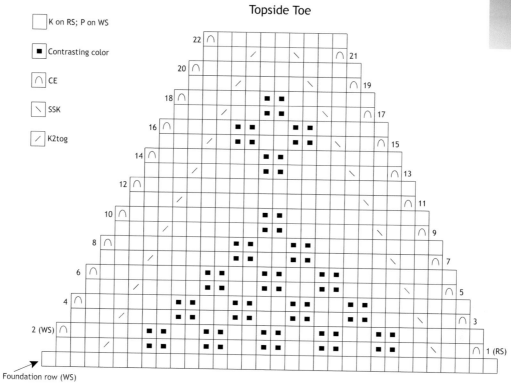

Foundation row (WS)

Last stitch to pick-up in CE before uniting to rnd

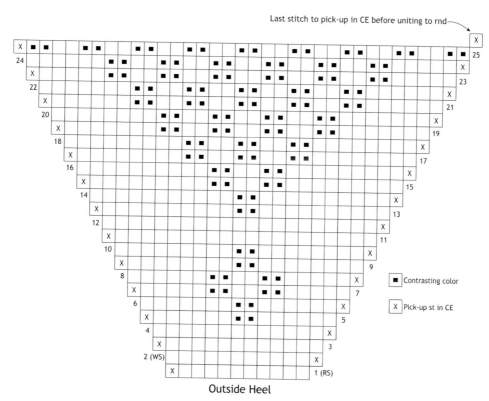

- ■ Contrasting color
- X Pick-up st in CE

Outside Heel

RESOURCES

Louet North America
3425 Hands Rd,
Prescott, ON, Canada
K0E 1T0
Phone: (613) 925-4502
(800) 897-6444
Fax: (613) 925-1405
info@louet.com

Plymouth Yarn Company, Inc
500 Lafayette Street
Bristol, PA 19007
(215) 788-0459
pyc@plymouthyarn.com

Blue Moon Fiber Arts®, Inc.
Socks That Rock
56587 Mollenhour Rd
Scappoose, OR 97056
(503) 922-3431 phone
(866) 802-9687 toll free
(503) 523-0092 fax
info@bluemoonfiberarts.com

Creatively Dyed Yarn
P.O. Box 1346
Greer, SC 29652
info@creativelydyed.net

Crystal Palace Yarns - Straw into Gold, Inc.
160 23rd Street
Richmond, California 94804
cpyinfo@straw.com

Ellen's 1/2 Pint Farm LLC
85 Tucker Hill Road
Norwich, VT 05055
(802) 649-5420
halfpintfarm@valley.net

Skacel Collection, Inc.
(800) 255-1278
info@skacelknitting.com

Cascade Yarns
Seattle, WA 98188
www.Cascadeyarns.com

Online Yarn
KLAUS KOCH GMBHRheinstrasse 19
35260 Stadtallendorf
www.online-garne.com
www.online-yarns.de

Babs Ausherman
Miss Babs: Hand-Dyed Yarns & Fibers
P.O. Box 78
Mountain City, TN 37683
(423) 727-0670
www.missbabs.com

Universal Yarns
284 Ann Street
Concord, NC 28025
(704) 789-Yarn (9276)
(877) UniYarn (864-9276)
www.universalyarn.com
Product Inquiries: sales@universalyarn.com

Sock Blockers by Rosemary "Chappy" Chapman
www.purrfectlycatchydesigns.com
thefisherman@rio-express.net
(309) 343-5323

Leslie Wind Knitting Jewelry
Clasps, Closures, Cable Needle Necklaces
www.lesliewind.com
(978) 546 6539

Specialty Knitting Bags
Barbara Parsons
(978) 281-1419
bg@ParsonsEtc.com

Strick-ly Socks

About the Author

Learning both music and knitting at the age of three, Candace Eisner Strick has followed these two loves all her life. Now retired from 16 years of teaching cello, she concentrates on designing, writing, and teaching knitting. She is the author of 7 books, her writing and designs have been published in every major knitting magazine in the country as well as in numerous compilation books by Vogue, Interweave, XRX, and Voyageur Press. She is the creator of her own line of yarn, Merging Colors, as well as her own line of patterns, *Strickwear*, which can be found in yarn stores and catalogs across the country, in Canada, and in the UK (*www.strickwear.com*).

Candace teaches workshops internationally at major knitting conventions and guilds. Her other fiber-related interests include spinning, weaving, dyeing and quilting. When not doing the above, she is riding her bicycle. She lives in rural Connecticut with her pianist/knitting husband Ken, a wonder-bunny, and a cockatiel. Both she and her husband are owned by a parrot. She has three grown sons, all of whom know how to knit but refuse to do so.

Notes